Journey of Faith

A Bridge Between God and Man

Richard A. Money

Ebook 978-1-304-89523-3

Softcover 9781628902440

Hardcover 978-1-304-89536-3

Printed in the United States of America

Table of Contents

Forward

If the reader has made it this far in the book you have my congratulations. The reason for the title will be explained later. I think this is what is known in some circles as "chumming the waters". I don't expect this book to be a record-breaking novel. In fact, the only reason it is being written is because so many people have told me over the years that I have a book in me. When am I going to get it out? Well, here it comes, for better or for worse. Where it will wind up and how, I have no idea. Like most of life, I trust that it will just happen as it is supposed to happen, even if I didn't always think that way. I really do believe that much of what has been written was written by a Power greater than me. I just am not that smart to have it otherwise. I have always said when people ask how I am, that "I am like fine wine. I get better with age!" I am not sure about that though, because age does not necessarily bring wisdom. It's just that people may be kinder to those of us who have some senility.

This book is comprised of many incidents in my life that I believe may show not what I have done, but what I have become with the Grace of God. If you are looking for a religious experience, I don't think you will find it here, although you may. I'm not making any promises.

I hope it is written simply and without any "axe grinding", but I'm sure there will be times when I just can't help myself. My opinions are important...at least to me. It is not my intention to disturb anyone. If the reader is satisfied with his or her present mode of worship or the religious manner in which they worship God, and if they have the Peace and Love in their hearts for their fellow man, then by all means this book is not for them. But if the reader is dissatisfied with what has been spoken to him or her and if they are searching for something that seems to be missing in his religion, then this book may inspire him to find a soul-satisfying element that has been missing. The Holy Spirit is still at work in the world, perhaps, even more today than in the past couple of hundred years.

This book does not contain all of the answers, but it may spark a fire which may lead to real Peace on earth and brotherhood for all men.

I hope you will find this journey of my life entertaining. Today, I wonder how I made it this far. I know it was by the grace of God and the Holy Spirit. And if the future of my life will be anything like the past, I know it will be a real HOOT! God really does have a sense of humor!

For all the events and people that have come into my life to make me what *I Am* today, I give thanks to the Supreme Power, God, or whatever you choose to call it. It is not that white-haired and balding old man sitting on a golden throne, but the Very Source of all. In All and with All. Past, Present and Future. Now on with the book or whatever.

PS. The balding old man with white hair is me. Any other similarity is purely coincidental or by His choice.

The Early Years

It was 1938. Hitler was invading Poland but I didn't care. I was busy being born to Richard and Mary Money. On March 2, Mom was giving me life in this world and seeing the light about which I will explain later. Dad was feeling no pain and I don't remember much about this memorable event either. Only Mom remembered the pain and let everyone know about it for almost ninety years. Especially me. I think there must have been a touch of Jewish mother in Mom. She loved guilt and didn't miss a chance to throw it out. It seemed like guilt and pain were her life's blood. More later.

Richard F. (Dad) was a complete orphan by the age of five. He was born in England of an English ship purser and an Italian woman named Sylvia Gogna. He lived in Italy in his early years with a grandfather and then in an orphanage until immigrating to this country when he was fifteen. He came by himself, by boat to New Orleans, and then traveled by train to St. Louis where he spent his entire life.

Upon arrival in St. Louis he did a variety of odd jobs, and as near as I can determine, living on the streets and working as he said "for food and a place to sleep." I have never heard of all the things he did to survive but I am sure his life was interesting in those years. A brother, Al, had immigrated earlier but could be of little help to Dad. He worked in a bank and had only recently married. There was little money for either of them.

It must have taken quite a bit for Dad to come to this country. He was the youngest of four children, three boys and a girl, and he never saw his oldest brother and his sister again in his lifetime. Communication was sparse between them and it was mainly Mom who encouraged him to write, which he seldom did. There was little family connection due to the fact that his father died when Dad was two and his mother when he was four. He was the youngest and had little memory of anyone except his grandfather.

In talking to some of the people that knew him, he was quite a character in those days, and definitely a ladies' man. At least until he met Mom. His nickname was Bronco. Now when I heard this for the first time I wasn't sure what it inferred, but I knew it wasn't defining Dad as a psalms–singing churchgoer. This was born out in later years. Of course since I was his firstborn son, and as I was told, his little companion, I was dubbed "little Bronco".

Mary (Mom) was born to Nicola Daniele and Dusolina Torrini in 1910 and, although born in this country, was conceived in Italy. Nick came to this country and went back to Italy for his wife and two other children. Mom was the youngest and seemed to lead a sheltered life as far as I can tell. She was working in a shoe factory when she met Dad. They met at a church club, and according to her, he was someone she didn't expect to fall in love with. I really don't think Dad was looking for a relationship with God when he met Mom either. I believe his sights were set on something more mundane.

Richard and Mary were married in 1934 at the end of the Depression. That Depression mentality stayed with them for the greater part of their lives, and to a degree, was handed down to their children. This wasn't all bad, but by today's standards it is a real oddity. We don't do without much today and if we have to, it isn't fair. We deserve everything we desire and we can't live without things.

When Mom and Dad met he was driving a truck for a grocery company, a job he held for almost forty five years. Apart from his odd jobs when arriving in this country, he drove a truck for all of his life. First he drove for an Italian import-export company and then for a full line grocery company.

My first impressions in this life were of salamis and cheeses hanging above a sawdust floor and huge barrels of olives with the smell of olive oil permeating everything. I remember being held by my feet by Dad over a barrel of olives and being allowed to grab all the olives that my little hands could hold. Heaven! To this day my children swear that I sweat garlic and olive oil. I think they are right. I lust for the stuff! These were the War Years, and although I wasn't aware of what really was going on, the atmosphere was tense. I remember the gold star being hung in windows and I knew this meant something important. I was more concerned with the iceman who came to deliver ice to my Grandmother's house. He came with a horse-drawn wagon, slinging a huge hunk of ice over his shoulder resting on a burlap sack and deposited it on the doorstep. This was put on the top tray of the little brown ice-a-box (as it was referred to by my Grandmother) to cool the food. Water collected on the bottom tray on a daily schedule. Freezers were as yet unheard of. The trick was to gather the shavings of ice as the iceman cut the huge twenty five, thirty, or even fifty pounds, which was to be delivered. Or, if we were really lucky we could ride on the back of the wagon as he moved to the next house.

The milkman had the same delivery routine. A horse-drawn wagon, but his horse was more intelligent. It would move to the next house by the milkman merely whistling. There was not an abundance of cars. Only a few had them.

We were lucky Dad had one, but it wasn't driven all the time. We only took the car out for Sunday rides and special occasions. Gas was rationed and although only 10 cents a gallon, it was hard to get.

We lived a few blocks from my Grandmother and Grandfather, my Aunt Louise and Uncle Fidelis and six first cousins. They all lived with my Grandpa and Grandma Daniels so it was easy to see almost the whole family at one time. My Aunt Julia and Uncle Louis, called Zia and Zio, were only a block away from Grandma and Grandpa's also. It was very convenient. The only family that was seen maybe once or twice a year was my Uncle Al's family, which consisted of his wife, Florence, and two daughters. They lived on the other end of town and were not seen except on the holidays. Grandpa was unemployed, and I think this was by choice. I only remember him working for a short time. He had better things to do. He would sit in the backyard and feed the birds and the squirrels. He would spend the fall months gathering nuts for the squirrels (as if they couldn't do it themselves) and feed corn to the pigeons.

The shed in the backyard of Grandpa and Grandma's housed a horse, which was owned by a ragman. This learned gentleman would traverse the alleys looking in ash pits and yelling "Rags, bottles, bones!" He housed his horse and wagon in the shed for a monthly rental fee. This was my first contact with rural life in the city. It was also my first contact with methane gas. Grandpa was well versed in the ways of nature and could tell when the horse (which at times was endowed with a great deal of flatulence) was about to release this gas into the atmosphere. He would quickly strike a match on his overalls and when placing it in the proper position behind that horse, we would all be treated to the wonders of a natural gas jet. Blue flame and all. What a wonder! Grandma did not think much of the trick at all.

Grandma spent most of her time in the kitchen, it seems. She would make a chicken soup that would curl the stomachs of most of the present populace. She made it out of fresh chicken and nothing was wasted. In went the head and feet and you could cut it with a knife if need be. But talk about healthy!

This was the fare recommended by their doctor to cure what ailed them. She would also make large loaves of polenta, which was cut with a string when it had cooled sufficiently. The Old World was always present and Italian was the language of both my grandparents. If I had known then what I know now, I would have learned the language. But Mom and Dad spoke English and since I was an American neither they nor I saw any need to speak Italian. To this day I can understand most of it, but have a difficult time speaking it.

I mentioned ash pits earlier. This was the Eighth Wonder of the World. To those who don't know what an ash pit is I will explain. It was a square concrete bin into which furnace ashes and garbage and whatever else one did not want was thrown. It was cleaned periodically by the ash or trash man who came in a wagon and hauled it away. The trick if you were a kid was to rummage through the pit before it was cleaned out and come up with the treasures that abounded there.

This could be an old alarm clock, picture frame, piece of pipe, old pot or pan, or even something that looked so good you couldn't pass it up even if you didn't know what it was. When it was brought home it had to be hidden for the most part or some adult would throw it in his or her own ash pit. Many ten-minute walks home from school would take almost an hour because the route was through alleys with frequent ash pit stops. I'm sure today that kids have lost this thrill.

Another wonderful event was the game of bottle caps. The local tavern would be contacted and a bag of bottle caps would be secured at absolutely no cost. These were thrown in such a way that they would dip, slice, or flare up depending upon the way they were thrown. The trick was to hit the cap with a boom stick thus constituting a hit. Just like baseball but there were no broken windows, etc. Today I don't believe a kid could go into a tavern without some fearing child endangerment, thinking that they only wanted a beer. The thought never crossed our minds that we could even desire a beer. That was for adults and we were too young at the time. However, things did change.

Now for cigarettes. That was something that was O.K., but they were hard to get. We had to satisfy ourselves with what was known to us then as "lady cigars." Catalpa pods. They were dried and cut into cigarette size and smoked with great relish. They tasted terrible but we thought they were really something. I remember the time that my Aunt Louise asked if we were smoking lady cigars. When we replied to the negative she calmly led us to the back porch and told us to look on top of the shed. We had carefully cut the pods, and looking for a place to dry them, laid them out symmetrically on top of the shed where they were quite visible to the naked eye from the second story where my cousins lived. We were undone. "We" most of the time was my older male cousin who was one of the six cousins with whom I spent most of my time.

Where I lived was, in those days, considered a very high-class place. The streets were lined with trees and the houses consisted of single-family dwellings and four family flats. We lived in a four family flat with three rooms, consisting of living room, bedroom, and kitchen. Very cozy, to say the least. I really wonder how Mom and Dad had more children after me. Maybe that is the reason for four-year intervals between us all...it took a lot of guts and a great deal of planning to do the DEED since everyone slept in the same room. I moved to the living room foldout couch when I was fifteen. Boy, my own room – complete with a television and living room furniture!! Until then I was on a cot and my sisters were in a bunk bed.

There was no one my age within a couple of blocks of us so I spent a lot of time by myself. Mom was very protective and I could not go more than six houses in ether direction from our front door. This was in a safer day than we live in today. I was twelve before I could cross a major street. My cousin was crossing it at nine. I was really embarrassed but Mom would not give in to my pleadings at letting me grow up by at least crossing the street.

The main entertainment in our home in those days was, of course, the radio. After supper Dad would sit back in the easy chair, and when Mom was finished with the dishes (as we got older my sister and I did them with a great deal of fighting, as I remember) she would sit in the living room with Dad. At about 7 p.m. the entire family would retire and turn on the radio in the bedroom. At 9 p.m. it would be shut off and we were all expected to dutifully go to sleep. Dad got up at 5 a.m., so when he went to sleep we all went to sleep.

I don't remember very many major traumas during those early years. I was not allowed to do very many things that other children my age were doing. First, there were not very many children my age, and secondly, Mom was very protective of me. Fighting with others was definitely not allowed, and even if I were picked on I would get in trouble if I fought back. Dad did not agree and taught me how to box. In fact, he even gave me a set of boxing gloves for my birthday when I was seven. The word got out in the neighborhood that the little Dago could not fight. So naturally, I was fair game. This did change after I disregarded my Mother's injunction and won a pretty good fight with a neighborhood bully. No one really bothered me too much again.

The major upset in those years came one Sunday afternoon when Mom and Dad and I went to an air show at Lambert Field. There was to be a demonstration of parachuting and some of the latest air equipment of the day that was winning the war. This was, I believe, 1943 or 1944. I remember this even so clearly that it seems like yesterday. The DC-3's came over the field and little white dots began to fall out from its sides. Paratroopers!! In real life! What a thrill and event for me. The excitement was building. Next on the program was to be a glider flight carrying the mayor and chaplain and some other dignitaries. A glider, of course, is an airplane without an engine. It was made of wood and towed behind a power-driven aircraft. When it was over its target, the towrope would be released and the glider would noiselessly glide to an open area delivering its cargo of men and machinery. It could not be picked up on radar because of its wooden construction and was becoming an important factor in the European war theater.

I can still see the dignitaries boarding the aircraft with the DC-3 taxiing down the runway, glider in tow. Both became airborne and flew away from the field becoming smaller as the distance increased. Then, circling, they began to head back to the field releasing the towrope as they passed overhead. As the rope fell from the glider's nose, and it separated from the airplane, something went wrong. One wing tilted crazily upward and began to drift down to earth while the main body of the craft began to spiral down erratically, crashing into the runway around fifteen thousand yards from were we stood. The impact threw pieces of wood and debris in all directions and it was evident even to this young mind that no one could have lived through this.

The screams of people all around me still echo in my ears, as much as the visual trauma hangs in my memory. This event left its impact upon me for many years and still plays a part in my dislike of flying. Mom was particularly hysterical, as I remember, for the next couple days, although Dad took a calmer attitude. I think it bothered him but he did not let on. His English heritage did not allow Dad to demonstrate much emotion or feeling. This was something that I had to learn over the years.

As I recall it was at about this time that I expressed desire to be Pope. It seems that Pope Pius XII was born in March and since my birthday was in March, I came up with the idea that this might be my calling. There was much laughter about it by Uncles, Aunts and Dad, but as I recall, Mom was almost ecstatic. Yes, she said, I certainly could be Pope. After all, I was Italian. Do you get the idea that Mom was sort of religious and bigoted in those days? I believe it was my Uncle Fidelis who said that the word was not pope, but spelled with two o's, and I had already made the grade. Mom did not care for this too much.

I don't know how many people remember Victory Gardens, but I do. This was part of winning the war by growing your own food so that the men overseas could be taken care of. We planted radishes, lettuce, and beans for sure, but I don't remember anything else that we could survive on. Looking back on it I believe it was more propaganda than a reality. We did have our own chicken that laid an egg now and then.

This, I really thought, was great. It was kept in the garage behind the house but I don't remember it lasting too long either. Dad was not much on livestock and pets. I wonder what became of it – Sunday dinner?

As far as food went, since there wasn't much refrigeration, most items were bought on a daily basis and it was pretty much fresh. Mom or Grandma would go to the market, which was several blocks away and purchase what was needed for the next few days. Meat was kept on ice, as were some other perishables. We had a small Crosley refrigerator that was electric, but it didn't hold much. I guess you could call it primitive by today's standards.

On Sundays my Zia and Zio, Julia and Louis, would sometimes take us to buy fresh produce and chickens directly from the farm. This was usually someone that Zio Louis knew and had fished in their pond or hunted mushrooms on their place. He was a great mushroom hunter. It seems that this was his main claim to fame – that and the fact that he could play the guitar in his underwear and sing Calabrese folk songs and drink at the same time. He was also very astute at catching pigeons on the roof of his house and had Zia Julia cook them for us kids. This was akin to having our own little chicken or turkey. It wasn't until later that I realized how bad they really tasted. It is amazing how childhood clouds reality at times.

I can still remember the red fat hens that were brought home from those trips to the country. They seem to represent the horn of plenty, and they were not treated lightly. Their demise was a wonder to behold. Grandpa would dispatch them with a twist of the wrist, which could seem cruel to some. Mom on the other hand, was much more delicate in her treatment of dispatch. She was only 4' 11" and not very heavily built. And according to her, she did not have the ability or moral fiber to be so cruel to a bird, even though it was to be a meal for her family. She, instead, would very delicately place a broomstick upon the hapless victim's neck, and then, grabbing its feet, stand on the broomstick yanking with a force that was worthy of King Kong. Needless to say, the chicken was a goner but it still provided us with the erratic flapping and bouncing, which to us kids, was the main event of the entire procedure. This activity of execution was carried on in the basement so no one could really know of my Mother's prowess with the broomstick. To this day I'm not really sure if she enjoyed it or merely acted the part of doing what needed to be done to feed the family.

The basement of our home was different from what one would call a basement today. It had a coal bin. Now, for those who have no knowledge of coal or how it was used, let me describe the coal bin, furnace, and concomitant paraphernalia. Coal came in various grades. There was the briquette, much like the charcoal briquette we buy today, and there was a larger chunk than the briquette. These two were relatively easy to shovel and handle. As such they were more expensive than the type that we could afford. This was the boulder size block of coal that needed to be broken up to fit in the furnace. These huge blocks of black rock were dumped in the street in front of the house, and it was up to the resident to put it in the coal bin. If you were rich, the coal man would wheelbarrow it to the coal bin for you. This was not our lot, of course. Dad would wheel the coal into the coal bin, with me helping in a very small way, since the coal was sometimes bigger than me (or so it seemed). When it was time to be used he would break up the large boulders with a hammer, sending coal dust all over. I'm sure it is a miracle that not one of us contracted black lung disease by this procedure.

The furnace itself was a huge monster with arms extending in all directions. These arms, as I learned later, were the air pipes that radiated the hot air through the house.

A fire was started with paper and wood, and then when they were burning sufficiently, lumps of coal would be shoveled upon it. Once caught, the coal would burn for several hours and as it burned it would leave its ashes in the bottom portion of the furnace. Hence, the ash pit was one of my first jobs around the house. "Take out the ashes" was the cry that would send terror through my body. It was heavy work and not like taking out the trash today that kids still hate doing even though it may only weigh a fraction of coal ashes. In later years the furnace was converted to oil and it did have a convenience to it, but those early furnace years could leave you with a sense of self-sufficiency. You had to always watch for the furnace going out (which then made it very hard to light again) because it didn't take long for the house to get cold. Even though it was banked at night, it needed to be attended to by 5 a.m. next morning and then again during the day. This was either Mom's or my job.

The hot water heater was something also. It was a round canister with tubing running circularly through it. It had a bank of gas jets and pilot light. When the pilot light was lit and the bank of jets ignited, the coil that contained water would be heated. This really did not put out a great deal of hot water fast, and baths with hot water were duly regulated. Most of the time water was heated upon the gas stove, one pot at a time. In those coal-burning days one of the most important things for a kid to remember was to scrape off the black dust before you ate the snow. I guess we have progressed in our environmental development, but in those days you could at least see what was not good for you.

I feel sorry for the folks who never experienced the pungent smell of piles of burning leaves in the gutters of the streets in the fall. It was not only a beautiful sight and one which brought neighbors outside to chat, but the pall of smoke did not smell half as bad as the diesel smoke prevalent today in our streets. I honestly don't think leaf burning was as bad as it is supposed to have been.

There is another thing that we miss today, the neighborhood gatherings on the front porches. Every evening after supper, weather permitting, the inhabitants of the houses and flats would sit on the front porch and exchange the events of the day. Perhaps one family would migrate to the neighbor's for the evening, and the next evening they would switch locations. The adults would sit on the porch while the children played catch in the street or on the sidewalk, or played tag and hide and seek. There was a sense of community that is not present today for the most part. Everyone knew who was where, and whose kid was whose, and what he or she was doing or what he or she was not supposed to be doing. The grapevine or jungle drums of the neighborhood could not be beaten for keeping a young hellion from raising Cain around the neighborhood. Talk about neighborhood watch! I remember thumbing my nose at Roseanne Capp a couple of houses up the street one day. Before the sun set, my Mother knew about it and I was chastised for doing something dirty. Can you believe it? I didn't even know what it meant but I was told what a dirty thing that was to do.

I wonder what would have happened to me if I had given her the bird!! (Of course, I had no idea of what that was either.)

There we lived was pretty close to the city limit. Six or seven blocks away were the beginnings of what we would call today, the suburbs. This consisted of small towns and houses with a lot of space between them. Not like where we lived. It seemed like once you got out of the city limit you were in the country. A block away from us was a family that had goats, and my earliest recollection in the mornings was being awakened by their bleating. This was an oddity and it didn't last too long as the neighborhood developed.

<u>Healing</u>

I have always wanted the gift of physical healing, just like a child wanting all the candy in the world. That is one of the major reasons for becoming a counselor or counseling psychologist. When the awareness came that we are Spirits having a Human experience and not the other way around, I realized that I would be a healer of the spirit or the mind and that would heal the body also. This is true, but it seems that I have also been given the gift of physical healing. This is hard for me to admit, but the Lord does use the strange things of this world to manifest His glory. (He couldn't find anyone stranger than me, that's for sure.) It had never really dawned upon me that the healing of the spirit is the most important element in the healing process, both physically and emotionally or spiritually. It has taken the writing of this book to realize fully what healing really means.

Jesus healed many people. Some got healed and left, never to be heard from again. Everyone wanted a physical healing in His time. Some were healed and began following Him. Some got the point on who He was and why He was manifesting the Father's Love. Others did not. His healings did not necessarily turn the healed to the Father because the healed person's spirit was focused, perhaps, on the physical and not the reason behind it. It seems that the reason for physical healing must be the healing of the spirit since we are spirits having this human experience.

A good friend and I were talking one day and he mentioned that the apostles were good salesmen. It hit me later (I didn't think much about it at the time) what he meant. They were selling Jesus to the world. Of course the Holy Spirit was helping them as the Spirit works through humans too. The miracles that Jesus manifested are not listed in all the gospels. There are some that seem to be related to Old Testament numbers. I believe that the Loaves and Fishes number may refer to the tribes of Israel. This does not mean that Jesus did not perform miraculous events all the time.

I don't believe miracles have to be instantaneous. They happen all the time. Look around at nature and wonder at the miracles taking place every season of the year. Consider the miracle of Life itself.

All healing is a healing of the spirit, no matter whether it is physical or emotional, for if it is a true healing the whole person is healed. We have all seen physically healthy individuals who are spiritually in need of a healing. Their personality or spiritual side is hurting and they can really be people we do not care to be around. We have also seen physically sick or diseased people whose spirits are absolutely beautiful and healthy and who manifest the goodness of God despite their physical pain or deformity or disease. I have been told that in my work, I, as it were, "cut to the chase" because I heal the spirit directly without concern for the body. This is not totally true because the healing must be integral. As the ancient Greeks said, "A sound mind in a sound body." This is what the ideal should be and is to be the goal of all healing.

Hopefully, the body and mind complement each other to result in a total healing.

In a physical healing the spirit must also be healed for it to be a genuine healing event. By that I mean that when the body becomes healed, the mind or soul or spirit must also have a healing that takes place. For example, if someone has a miraculous healing take place in his or her body, the spiritual healing might be that there is a greater awareness and proclamation of the glory of God's goodness. This could even be manifested by the person changing his attitude toward his fellow man (e.g., they become more kind and compassionate). Therefore, ALL healing is directed to the goal of becoming more Godlike.

Often times people noted for their healing ability declare that the one seeking the healing must have faith that they will be healed. I feel that this is erroneous. FAITH IN A GOD THAT CAN HEAL OR NOT HEAL IS NECESSARY but not in a GOD WHO HEALS EVERY TIME HE IS CALLED UPON.

A great amount of guilt is laid upon individuals who are told that since they are not healed they didn't have enough faith. This is the minister's cop-out. I also feel that it isn't necessary to scream and holler when praying for healing. It is related, at times, that when Jesus healed he sighed, looked to heaven and asked the Father for the healing. I don't think he screamed and hollered at anytime for the healing, but what do I know! I didn't realize that spiritual healing was more important than physical. Both are important, only one is necessary.

In praying with a man for the physical healing of lung cancer which seemed to be leading to imminent death, I saw the lung cancer tissue renew itself, and one would think that this would be the physical healing desired. Wrong. Instead of the cancer being eliminated the man I prayed with found peace within him and desired to go on to the other side, dying peacefully in the transition, telling me ahead of time that I had done my job because he was ready to meet the Lord. Had my prayer failed? No. It did achieve the purpose for which it was allowed to be by the Lord.

Of course, in my naiveté or basic ignorance, I felt that I had failed. But the Lord forgives me – I'm new at the game! This was an actual case, and I learned a lot from it.

In another case, the person was so depressed and had no incentive to live that death seemed to be right around the corner. For months he had lain in a hospital bed unable to move and really didn't care about anything. The depression, of course was mental or emotional, but the fact of immobility was physical. After several months of weekly prayer, and sometimes twice a week, the patient began to move his limbs, imperceptibly at first, but then more and more until he was in a wheelchair and going home.

This patient and I had been friends for years and we knew each other pretty well. One day after praying with him, he opened his eyes and declared that he had seen the Light. I looked at the window and seeing that the shades were drawn, told him so. He declared emphatically and in no uncertain terms, " THE LIGHT, STUPID! THE LIGHT!!!!!"

From that time on I was certainly being educated by the LORD in healing prayer. I really am a slow learner. Thank God He uses dummies.

Speaking of dummies let me tell the conclusion of this healing event. Pat, the patient, did go home and was very happy about it. Life became somewhat normal for him, which is what he desired. I hadn't heard from him for a couple of months, so one day I called him and got the answering machine. It was his voice on the machine so I left the message, "Well, you sound like your old self. I am happy to see you are not dead! Call me when you can." I got a call back from his wife, Judy, who informed me that Pat had died in his sleep LAST NIGHT. He had a heart attack and was very peaceful. Even I couldn't believe the Lord would allow this dummy to do what I did!!

The events (beginning to pray with people) began three years ago when I went to a seminar with two friends of mine who were also desirous of having a healing ministry. I had really not given physical healing much thought for the past several years. A lot of years in fact.

This was to be something new, my friend thought, and was sure that the Lord wanted him and me to attend this seminar in Kansas City. I finally relented and decided to go after some promptings from the Lord, I think. The seminar was on how to get into the energy of the person being prayed with, releasing the energy that brings healing, something of that nature. No words were to be spoken and this was not to be any religious experience for the one praying or the one being prayed with. During the course of the seminar and in the hands-on experiences there were some feelings of energetic movement. Basically, I was not impressed but I had heard of this type of energy healing and thought it might be useful in my therapy practice. I did make some adjustments to it which I will reveal very quietly. I USED THE NAME OF JESUS AND

PRAYED IN HIS NAME TO THE FATHER!!!! This was after I left the seminar and was on my own.

On the way home from the Kansas City seminar, I visited my son and daughter-in-law who, a couple of weeks earlier, had their first-born son.

Since the delivery was horrendous my daughter-in-law was still in terrible pain throughout her entire body. An OB friend of mine, who I consulted with about the situation, declared that there could be months of pain before she would feel better. This was not the good news I was looking for. When I got to my son's home, my daughter-in-law was still in bed, where she had spent the last several weeks, unable to do much of anything. "Well," I thought, "why not give the stuff I had just been exposed to a try." I began to move my hands over her body at a height of about six to eight inches. Moving from the top of her head to the tip of her toes and at times making a circular motion as I had been shown.

Nothing happened. No miracle here. Even though I had invoked the name of Jesus and had asked the Father in His Name and in the name of the HOLY SPIRIT to heal this woman, it didn't work. I had given her some hope, but no cigar. Just as I thought, I didn't have the gift. I gave everyone a hug and left for home.

That was Sunday evening and on Monday I heard nothing. On Tuesday my son called and said Carolyn, my daughter-in-law, wanted to speak with me. It seemed that on Monday she had no pain and was so normal that she didn't think much about it until her mother asked how she was feeling. That is when it hit her that the prayer worked. WOW!!! I didn't know what to think but praised God and I was truly amazed even more than anyone else. I guess I can be a doubting Thomas too.

But in my defense, this was the first occasion that a healing actually took place. From that time on the confidence has been building. Not in my own ability, but in the belief that I have been around when the LORD had worked HIS WONDERS. It is a very humbling experience for me. I am sure it will always be humbling for me to see God work. My faith needs building constantly and He knows it.

Shortly after this experience, perhaps within a few months, I was at a family gathering with most of the family. Grandchildren were all over the place, or so it seemed. One of the youngsters was running along the poolside when he slipped and fell, hitting his elbow.

I was inside and did not see it happen, but when his mother carried him in and sat him down, I could see the elbow swollen already to the size of a baseball. At the time, I must admit that something possessed me to tell her to let me hold him. She did so, and I put my hand on Garrett's swollen elbow while she went to get ice because she thought it might even be broken. Within seconds, but at the most a minute, the swollen elbow lost the swelling and became normal sized. My daughter-in-law was sitting across from me and her eyes were as big as saucers. She had witnessed it also. Again, WOW! In about ten minutes my grandson was outside by the pool playing as if nothing had happened. My life was beginning to change. Here was proof that I may not have done fantastic miracles, but something was indeed going on in my life. Healing touch? I don't care what you call it, God is around and doing something. Again, I am honored. There have been more healing touch experiences, e.g. frozen thumb moving, touch on the forehead to relieve fever and some things which I cannot remember at this time. They may seem to be small to some, but to me the manifestation of God's Power is always a humbling thrill.

I have felt more like a healer in my counseling. In counseling psychology, the healing of the spirit of the person or the soul is very satisfying. When the spirit is healed the person is really healed and it is not just a matter of physical activity. The symptoms are not considered as much as the mind is healed which prevents the symptoms from overtaking the person. It seems to me that this is what Jesus was most concerned with. He healed the spirit of the person by declaring that we are all children of One God, the Father. If we were always aware of that fact then the symptoms and the diseases of the world and of relationships would be nil.

The healer's job then is to actually become more like Jesus. The main thrust of the healing is to reveal the Father and His mercy to the individual, just as it was the primary focus of the life of Jesus. We have believed, it seems that the main or primary reason for Jesus was a healing ministry of the sick of the world.

This may not be the case. We have focused on His miraculous healings which may or may not have occurred depending upon the writer's perspective. If the Father wills it, the miraculous healing will take place. This is evident when Jesus always asks the Father first when He prays for a person. When the Father wills it the miraculous healing takes place. When He does not, the miracle does not take place. This is another reason for some people being miraculously healed and some not. The job of the healer, then, is still to reveal the Father and His Fatherhood to all men, and to pronounce that all men are to be children of the One God. We are not children of the evil in the world.

Miraculous healing does not change a person interiorly or perfect their spiritual life of necessity. Some are healed of their afflictions and still do not accept at a later time the Fatherhood of God.

We sometimes forget what happened by the momentary joy of the healing process. Miraculous physical healing need not to be the primary focus of the healer, but the acceptance of the fact that God alone is the Father and healer the primary focus is the turning of the healed soul to God the Father. Looked at this way, it is evident that miraculous healing can be a detriment to the real reason for a healing, and that reason is the turning of the soul to the Father. Sometimes people may focus on the physical to the detriment of the spiritual. This may be the reason that working wonders cannot be foremost in individuals turning to God. Is it possible that some of the miracles attributed to Jesus were not miraculous healings but somehow natural events that were mistaken by the apostles as miracles? Everything that Jesus said and did was to demonstrate to all that the One God, His Father, was the Father of us all. In that contains the reasoning that we are all brothers as children of One God.

BOTTOM LINE: No one knows why one is healed and another is not, for no one knows the mind or mystery of God.

When we pray for a healing, we desire to see the results with our human minds, but we must allow for the fact that the healing may take place in the spiritual realm which we cannot see.

God answers every prayer one way or the other. Of course, we get humanly excited when it is done OUR WAY. This does not always happen and we must remember that HE IS GOD and knows what the person needs. THEREFORE, we pray as if everything we desire depends upon us...but knowing all the while that all the results depend upon God!!!

Some of the events described above are my feeble attempts to figure out the healing process and what we need to do. These miraculous healings did not take place instantly, and, in fact to my childish way of thinking initially, *I* felt that *I* had failed. In some, the spirit was healed first and then the physical. In others it was the other way around. Notice I used the word "*I*". This is totally wrong, for it is never the *I*. Healing is always done by God, never by man. The man is merely present when God may choose to work miraculously. The reality of the situation is that I really don't know. I wish I did, but let's face it – we live in a salami factory where not much is really known for sure.

<u>Call to the Seminary</u>

After graduating grade school with all the blessings of the nuns, since I was to be trained as a priest, I proceeded to enroll at the St. Louis Prep Seminary which was located at the other end of the earth. I entered the seminary at fourteen years old against my father's advice. He wanted me to go to CBC (Christian Brothers College) or some other school so that I could be normal – dating like other high school kids and not being pressured with the burden for my age of setting my sights on being ordained twelve years down the line. Mother, on the other hand, was ecstatic. She would have a priest in the family and she would be guaranteed salvation, which I found out later, was even in the dogma of the Roman Church. It was not definite, but with a pretty sure chance of it happening for her. I felt that I would give it a try and if I didn't like it, I would and could quit and go to a secular school.

Becoming a priest was a very desirable goal, but I really didn't care much for the fact that priests could not marry. But, oh well, I was fourteen and it didn't seem so bad then. Even though I felt I did want a family. Besides, one of my best friends had gone for a year and he said it was great. So I gave it a try.

We lived in a four family, three-room flat in the northwest quadrant of the city, and the seminary was in the southwest quadrant of almost St. Louis County. It took three buses and walking a mile to get to the high school which required getting up at 5 a.m., going to Mass (which was mandatory) by walking six blocks, walking to the bus stop, getting on the first bus, then the second, then the third, walking a MILE literally, and arriving at school by 7:30 a.m. Classes were over around 3 p.m. and then the procedure reversed, arriving home around 4:30 p.m. Talk about going to the little schoolhouse in four feet of snow! The old timers didn't have anything on us. If the buses didn't run because of the weather, it wasn't the school's fault. If we didn't make it and they didn't call off school for lack of attendance we were marked absent.

Compassion was hard to come by in those days! Some days the administration called off school after most of the students had arrived. If it took one hour on normal days, with snow it took almost three hours (six hours back and forth!). This really tested one's desire for seminary training.

The Preparatory Seminary was just that, a prep high school that prepared one for the actual priestly training. I lived at home, worked during the summers, and hung around with neighborhood friends. My life was pretty normal except for no dating girls which I didn't have time for anyway and no real desire to do so. During the summers I first worked for a grocery store stocking shelves. The next year I turned 16 and got a job working in a plating factory. My first real experience with Neanderthal Man! Not everyone was like that but there were enough young men having no education and schooling to begin working when legal, that it really was an education in the baseness of young men.

I was not a prude, mind you, but there was more cursing, dirty talk, actions and vile language than I was used to hearing. I had ridden on the truck with my father since I was seven years old and I thought I had heard it all. Nope. This was the beginning of my real education. It also seemed like fighting was the preferred procedure after work. It didn't take much to get a match going; a word, a look, or no word or look. It didn't make any difference. The alley would fill at the end of the day. Bets would be made on who the victor would be at the end. Though I never stayed at work for the festivities, I would know the next day by the bruises, black eye, or cuts on the face who was the winner.

I was not really expected to stay and watch or join in the festivities because I was known as the "PREACHER" and was not expected to either know how to fight or was too big of a chicken to do so. They may have been right on both counts and it made me very happy! Then one day my string of good luck came to an end. Someone dared a gentleman (?), who I will leave unnamed to pour water down my boot. "See what the preacher will do." became the war cry.

Now if the reader has ever been in a plating factory, it is a planetary hell including the temperature, nothing but water, acid, and steam everywhere on good days. That year, 1954, the temperature outside in August was 114 degrees. Inside, it was 140 degrees. This was a bad day and getting worse for me, for the water carrying gentleman from Illinois knew how to fight in a cesspool. We all wore boots and rubber aprons and gloves and, though the water would have been welcomed to my feet, this was a matter of principle.

This gentleman and took a bucket of water and began to approach me. Tauntingly, he asked me what I was going to do. He had such an aura of confidence that I replied with forced bravado. "I'm going to knock you on your ass". That did it. He approached and lifted the bucket. At that moment I swung, knocking him off balance and he fell on his ass, much to the laughter and applause of the crowd. Now I WAS in DEEP DOO DOO. He got up swearing that tonight I would meet him outside in the alley and I would see what would happen. My goose was cooked.

I had no big ring or roll of quarters to fill my hands. I really didn't feel like being hamburger, either. Then the Holy Spirit took over.

There was an old man who had worked there since he was sixteen and was now twenty four. His name was Jack, a fellow Mediterranean. He was the acknowledged leader and best fighter of the entire pack of teen-aged wolves. He, in a very compassionate manner, told the water boy that if he touched me again or pushed me into a fight, he would have his ass kicked like never before. The fight was over and Jack became a life-long friend, even attending my ordination Mass. To this day I think of him often especially when I can bite into steak or chew gum.

Life in the seminary when I boarded in senior year was not the most uplifting event in my life. To board at school was better than riding and hitchhiking for three or four hours a day, but it did cramp my style. It was all on-schedule for classes, for eating, drinking, playing, and anything else you may have to do.

We had to write out and submit our schedules to the dean and then make any adjustments that were suggested. Once we arrived at the school in September it was a lock-down until Thanksgiving when we could go home for four days. No home visits of any sort unless someone died. No one could visit at the school unless they were called for disciplinary purposes. Christmas vacation was approximately two weeks. Easter was a one-week vacation. Finally, the end of the year and home for three months, almost.

Of course, the three month vacation was a working vacation for me. I needed to work to pay the tuition. I had paid for my books and tuition since the beginning of my high school days. That's not to say that Mom and Dad didn't help me when I got in a bind, and they did keep most clothes on me. I do remember one time being in dire need due to an emergency situation that arose in one of my college years. I had a good friend a year older than me who liked to play the horses. And although he did work during the summer months, he made more money at the racetrack than at his job. In fact, one year he bragged that his tuition was totally paid by track betting. I was never, and am still not, a betting person (unless it is a sure thing) but at the end of the summer of this year in question he and I went to the racetrack.

Every summer most of us working stiffs kept a small stash aside for a night out or a vacation before school started. This particular year I had around seventy dollars, enough for books and then some. Books were going to cost around forty dollars, so I had enough to play with. Or so I thought.

My friend cautioned me early on not to bet with him. Even though he normally won more than he lost he did have bad nights. Guess what... this was one of his worst. Not to mention it was a disaster for me! I bet with him all the way, hoping that he would come out of it. After all, I knew nothing of racing except you could make money. I not only blew the mad money, I blew the book money too. There was no way to make up the almost forty dollars for the books.

With my tail between my legs, I fessed up to my Mother on what I had done. I really did not want to face Dad, who I knew would be really angry for my lack of self-control and faulty reasoning and would probably say; "Tough. Go talk to your mother." Of course, Mom did dip into the cookie jar and save the day, and I really learned a valuable lesson. When you earn a dollar take responsibility for how you spend it.

The Healing Process

We are made in the image and likeness of God. Therefore anything God can do, I can do. Right? No, but not altogether wrong. I am not "The God", but he has granted me the use of His power. There is only One Principle, One Power, One Process, One God. It is only One, but I reflect to Him what He is. Without me working in the world, He has His hands tied behind Him, as it were. At this point we are not considering Jesus and the Holy Spirit but only the power of healing brought by them both.

Healing can take many forms. There are spiritual, physical, emotional, and psychological healings and they do not depend on either healer or the one being healed. Faith in God does not always absolutely depend upon the faith of the person being healed or again the faith of the healer. If this were the case, people with great faith in God would always be healed.

I don't think this really happens all the time, although it can. We observe at times that those with great faith are not visibly healed as they would hope and pray for, even though they have believed and prayed and have given it to God.

Some don't believe in healing and yet they are healed. They may receive a healing through medicine, or perhaps a miraculous event which they attribute to chance, but in either manner they are healed. What then really comprises the HEALING PROCESS? I believe it is really a mystery that cannot be solved by mankind on this planet. I do not think that it can be logically dissected but the results are evident when someone is healed. It is not only by prayer, nor is it only by faith or intention, or circumstances alone that the healing takes place. It is a mysterious Process, and the key word here is Process. We can know what it is not, but it is much harder to say what it is.

Is it only in the giving up to God in total abandonment and submission that no matter what is happening only God is in charge? Yes. Is it not only believing that God is a loving father who has only our good in mind, no matter what it looks like to us at the time? Yes. Is it not only in the collective unconscious of mankind and in the individual that the total abandonment to God gives a peace beyond all understanding that no matter what happens, God is in charge as that Loving Father? Yes. Well, then, there is nothing left for man to do in this world except give it all to God. This does not really solve the Mystery, however.

It is in depth of the UNKNOWING where the depth of faith and union with God is revealed. This is the Mysterious Process. It is the UNKNOWINGNESS that cannot be known in this world and yet binds the soul to its maker. It is the trust without evidence, the faith that is not seen. It is the Unknown Process which is visible and yet not visible to the eye and, at times, even hidden to the mind.

The dependence upon God is not the only element in the healing process, in either the healer or the one being healed. What does make a difference in the Process of healing is the Inner Peace, which results from the acceptance of God as a loving Father.

What may seem to be primary is the Peace that affects both the healer and the one being healed. WHAT IS... JUST IS...and GOD IS ALL THERE IS. How often we have said "LET GO AND LET GOD." Let the Mysterious Process be and the good and Peace will also exist. It may not be evident, but it will still exist. It will still be and it will happen. We call this, perhaps, a curing process. It is unseen, but nevertheless, it will have its effects. These effects are acceptance, peace, and gratitude bestowed by the Mystery of the Process Itself. Let's look at this in a natural or physical manner of speaking. Let us look at this as compared to the making of a salami (or any other sausage if the reader is so inclined.) Since I am of Mediterranean descent, I am partial to salami.

We first take meat; either pork or beef and most of the time both, grind it up and allow for the fat. Fat is part of the meat and really adds flavor. Could it be that all of mankind is the various meats? Of course, we all have fat so leave it in by all means. That is, unless you're a vegetarian; but if that's the case you won't be making salami anyway.

We then take the various spices, such as garlic (the most important one), then salt, pepper, and other spices known only to the Italian salami maker who cannot divulge them under pain of death. Other spices from other cultures are allowed but they should all contain garlic in my viewpoint.

These spices, which can be looked upon as the various events in life, or even the emotions of joy, pain, depression, fear, anxiety, anger, etc., are then added to the meat of life and ground up again to make sure the blend of everything courses throughout the meat. This could be looked upon as all of mankind in this world. This mix of meat and spice is then stuffed into a casing that holds it all together. It is then hung up to cure at the proper temperature. Here, then, is the mysterious element. Nothing changes to the naked eye, but the salami in the curing process begins to take on a special flavor. It is an internal process of enzyme change. To me, I would call it a spiritual maturing process, again, much like mankind on this earth. It is an internal activity which is also required of men in relationship to the Father.

It seems to me that we are all salamis curing to become Godlike. The curing process of the physical salami makes it the Italian ambrosia of the world at large.

The spiritual curing of all men, or the process of the mystery of healing, makes all mankind the Beautiful Essence of God the Father. The purpose of life on this planet is to cure, and Jesus is the Great Salami Maker along with the Holy Spirit. No disrespect intended, but written from the soul.

College Years

I have described the high school years to a degree. High school was just that until the senior year where we were allowed to wear the Roman Collar and cassock (the dress). This was kind of a major event. It meant we were getting close to the desired goal – the priesthood, yet so far a distant purpose.

We were the first class of Cardinal Glennon College, which meant we would attend the school with college courses for four years, and then move to Kenrick for Theology. Until this time it was St. Louis Prep Seminary for six years, and then six years of theology at Kenrick. To achieve this task it would be required of our class, being the first, to acquire accreditation from the North Central Accreditation Association. This was a monumental task, which required us to take twenty six credit hours each semester. The pressure was incredible. Some students couldn't take it and cracked up. Others just quit. I got by with minor injuries, mainly using aspirin and coffee during exam time.

Of course, this did not give me the desired high that I needed to stay awake for studying, but I found it to be a sleep inducing diet. As soon as I drank a cup of coffee and swallowed some aspirins I immediately fell asleep. I wish that were the case today. I guess fifty years makes the difference. Nevertheless, I made it through.

We had half days of school on Wednesday and Saturday – time to relax after you did the chores like cleaning the toilets, working on the outside crew, or some other tasks, which were determined by the sadistic administration. I lucked out; since I loved the outdoors I volunteered for the outside crew which meant cutting wood and delivering the firewood to residents who paid $40.00 a truckload. This was done during free time on Saturdays. This was really a fine job, because there was always a way to sneak home and grab some decent food and a beer. What a treat since there was no way to escape except to go over the hill. The way out was to cut wood and be given transportation at the same time!!! I took full advantage of this, as did several other cunning friends.

It was also at this time that I learned to drive a tractor. This was a lifelong dream and I really enjoyed it. The outside crew was supposed to be the toughest but, believe me, it had its advantages! I really think it saved my college life. I would even give up the soccer games on the days off to deliver wood. Boy, was I dedicated – and getting fatter all the time with Mom's cooking. Not to mention a few beers. Oh, how I mortified myself!

At this time we were also clearing about two hundred acres for a golf course, which I found out later was not really for golf, but to raise the price of the acreage that was being sought for subdivisions. Never let it be said that the Roman Catholic Church was not thinking at this time. Along with the clearing and plowing came certain privileges which of necessity meant going into town for equipment repair, always passing Steak and Shake or something else.

Apart from the Bible classes, the courses were pretty much standard college courses as I remember.

The time went by pretty fast and the outside crew stood me in good stead for summer work at the seminary, doing pretty much what I did during the year, but during the summer I got paid for it. At least, that's what they called it. It sure beat working in a plating factory. Up to this time I had one other job that did pay pretty well for summer work. I was a hotshot delivery person for Buss Fuse Company. When there was a breakdown in a factory and they needed fuses fast, it was me that got the car to deliver the goods. I also picked up corporate executives at the airport. I really did like this job. The only reason I got it was because I was inept with a slide rule and a micrometer in the lab. Too bad.

After finishing college, Kenrick Theological Seminary was the next step. Here it was – the Big Time. Getting closer to the Priesthood. Courses in Bible, Moral Theology, Liturgy, and Dogma. Four years to go. The Order of Acolyte was first, and then Tonsure, next the Subdeaconate, then the Deaconate, and finally the twelve years would culminate in the Priesthood itself.

I was getting closer to what I had always dreamed of and the studies were more exciting and interesting, at least most of them, if not all.

It was during the second year of Theology that Life magazine came out with the news that a priest in Italy had been allowed to marry. This was to be an event that he had been sworn to secrecy to never reveal. He revealed it anyway and what a stir it made among us forced celibates! A lot of the conversations were about the why and necessity of celibacy. It really had no connection except a historical one that had been in use for the past four hundred years. Suddenly there was hope that I could be a priest and still get married and have a family. To be sure, the authorities did all they could (and it was considerable) to squash any hope of the law of celibacy being changed. Nevertheless, celibacy became a hot topic among the seminary students. Really nothing in my life changed. I was resigned to the law and I had made up my mind to live with it, as did others. Or at least I thought so.

It never did make much sense to me, but it went with the territory and I didn't have any trouble with it at this time. Besides, I was the KING OF THE HILL. I had been made head sacristan and was in charge of supplying the teachers with vestments and setting up the numerous altars for their daily Mass. I was also in charge of disposing of the wine left in the cruets after they had finished Mass. This part of the job I was especially conscientious about. And somehow, I became the chosen friend of many fellow students who never paid any attention to me before. Don't misunderstand. I am not now nor have I ever been an alcoholic. But being isolated for nine months every year for at least eight years, a sip of wine before breakfast was a real treat, sought after by many.

The job of sacristan also gave me the opportunity to drive the staff car to the St. Louis Cathedral during Holy Week to set up the services for the then Cardinal Ritter. A very prestigious job and a car to boot! A lot of responsibility but a lot of benefits too.

Richard A. Money

As I write this, it sounds very childish to me, but the reader must remember that at twenty-five to twenty-six years old, we had little outside contact. We were not even allowed to have a radio in our room or to keep up with most of the news of the day. Looking back on it God must have been in charge of me getting ordained, because I don't believe any one would put up with this today. DIVINE PROVIDENCE.

At this time Pope John the XXIII had convened the Second Vatican Council which opened the windows of the stolid and stale Roman Church, and some changes were taking place, even among our professors. The dean of students knocked on my door one evening and caught me listening to my contraband radio. It was about two months from ordination and freedom. He could have stopped my ordination, which I heard had been done in the past, but he chose to ignore it. He merely looked at me and smiled, told me what he needed to tell me and left. I began to breathe again ten minutes later! This was the same dean and liturgy professor who asked me why I was holding my hands the way I was when practicing the Mass. They were to be held shoulder high not higher, and even with the body. If it was done any other way it was a mortal sin if done on purpose, but only venial if it was accidental. I responded by pointing out the instructions in the liturgy book, and he responded BUT WHY ARE YOU DOING IT? I said with great aplomb, "I DUNNO, THE BOOKS SAYS TO DO IT". He asked me how would I do it? I replied with arms raised and outstretched as the prophets of old did it. He then said, "Do it the way you want. Just have a reason for doing it." THIS WAS THE BEGINNING OF THE END FOR ME. A REASON TO DO THINGS NOT BECAUSE YOU WERE TOLD TO, BUT TO AT THE VERY LEAST BE REASONABLE, AND NOT DO IT BECAUSE IT HAS BEEN DONE FOR FOUR CENTURIES!!!!!!!! Yes, the Church was changing and it seemed for the better. Non-Catholics could now get to heaven with Catholics. You could eat meat on Fridays. Fasting was becoming optional and even the Mass was going to be said in English. (Could it be that people would understand what they are praying to God?) And wonder of wonders,

Mass could be said facing the people.

These were some of the changes that were in front of me as I was going to be ordained. Things were looking up. Perhaps celibacy would be done away with also, and I was not the only one praying for that one, I know. (By the way, most of the priests who trained us during that time also left the priesthood to marry.) It was said at this time that the Pope had opened the windows of the Catholic Church for the first time in centuries and there was a great deal of excitement about the changes that could be taking place. All the time spent learning Latin didn't seem to matter if you could begin to pray in your native tongue without looking up what you were saying. I know some people to this day prefer the Latin Mass, but I feel this is purely an emotional attachment to a childhood ritual.

We really were isolated from September to June except for Thanksgiving Holiday (three days), Christmas Holiday (two weeks), Easter (about a week as I remember), until June when we were released. I use the word "released" because it was like getting out of jail, unless you were being punished by having to do some time in the dorm.

We each had our own room which consisted of a washbasin, a desk, a bed, and a built in locker. It even had a window where you could look out at the real world, and long for release. The general rule was no talking in the halls except during recreation time, and definitely not before morning prayers or after evening prayers. Sign language was discouraged but allowed.

The day started at 5:10 a.m. by what the faculty called the "voice of God." This was the first time that I began to have doubts about God. Anyone that could make that much noise so early in the morning couldn't be an occupant of heaven! It was a huge bell that I am sure woke up the entire neighborhood, and woe to the poor soul whose room was within ten feet of this wall monster. Morning prayers began at 5:30 a.m., and I mean began promptly. If you were not in the pew by then you definitely heard about it. If you happened to wake up sick you had to dress and check in with the dean, who never did sleep, but who stayed awake all night waiting for latecomers or the sick and lame. If you were sick enough you could go back to bed. Granted this was a necessary evil, because when waking up at that time and being expected to pray was enough to make anyone feel the urge to hibernate for the day. I was pretty lucky. When I woke up I hit the floor running. I was used to the time due to the fact that I had to get up at that time to ride the bus to school. I have still been doing it whether I need to or not.

Meditation was from about 6:15 a.m. to 6:45 a.m. when Mass would begin, or maybe it was 6:30 a.m., I really don't recall exactly. I do know that if you were caught dozing off or snoring while meditating there was a prompt response from the dean by banging you on the head with a prayer book or Bible. Most of us felt the Word of God at some time or another. After morning Mass there was a short time for more prayer of thanksgiving and then breakfast. This was a real treat.

Until my days at the seminary I did not know eggs could be green. Most of the time there was cereal and, as I remember, fried or scrambled eggs for breakfast.

Once in a while, especially on Sundays, there would be bacon or sausage. The eggs, as I say, were tinged with a green cast to them. They were either old or they were laid by Irish chickens. The nice thing about a fried egg, you didn't have to use a utensil to put them on your plate. They just slid off the plate along with about two ounces of grease. When a complaint about this was made to the cook, Sister Zita responded that grease was good for you, it kept you regular. Boy was she right! We were all just plain old regular students most of the time, believe me.

After breakfast followed the regular school day schedule. Classes were over about 2:30 p.m. and then there was recreation time. As I remember and I could be wrong, we had to be back in our rooms for a study period at about 4:30 p.m. or 5:00 p.m. or thereabouts. Then we had a little more prayer and dinner at 6:00 p.m. There was again no talking for the first fifteen minutes of any meal. It was a time for spiritual books to be read to us for the first part of the meal and then we could talk for the second half of the meal.

This was followed by an hour of free time, which was mostly spent walking around the campus or playing pool or ping-pong or just smoking in the lounge. Thank God smoking was allowed in certain areas in those days because I do think that we could have gone stir crazy without it! Night prayers followed at 7:30 p.m. and then study until 10:00 p.m. when there was lights out. This is where you learned to read under a blanket by a flashlight or listen to a transistor radio, or even a crystal set attached to a water pipe as I had. I bet someone reading this (probably a modern seminarian) does not even know what a crystal set is.

This was all not completely a time without some fun and humor. Perhaps a little childish humor, but after all we were children until ordained at twenty six years old. At that time we were cut free and became mature adults or so we were led to believe. There was a favorite game played at the dining room table when several people would be sitting at the table (it was a table consisting of twelve occupants, six and six to a table which was pushed together).

One of the people sitting at the end of the table would lift the tablecloth hanging over the edge, fill it with water, and with the help of the one or two people sitting down the line, allow the water to flow down the trough onto the lap of the hapless and unsuspecting victim. Since this was done in silence, the victim would just sit through the ordeal with wet pants. Anything for a laugh was the motto in order to keep sane.

Sports, especially soccer, hoc-soc, basketball, handball, and tennis, were foremost in order to keep one rational. Everyone was encouraged to participate in something. There was not much else to do except read and study and smoke. In order to make sports more interesting, nationalities were formed to increase the competition. It was Irish against German most of the time. It didn't make any difference if you were neither Irish nor German – you had to be one or the other. Since I had some Irish blood I was, of course, always on the Irish team. Major games of touch football and soccer were played on Sunday afternoons. If you were not playing you had another interest like reading or just hanging around to while away the free time. I think we were even allowed to listen to the radio. Since soccer was primary in a parochial school, this was the main sport along with hoc-soc. Hoc-soc today would be compared to indoor soccer, but it had a completely different flavor in the seminary days.

The game was played in the gym that had three walls with no opening whatsoever. There was a small area where the ball could get out of the playing field, but it was limited. It was legal to play the ball off the wall with bank shots or whatever. Even the ceiling was fair play. The goal was as big as a hockey goal and there were five players. Sometimes there may have been six players, but this was not the normal number if my memory is correct. The game was really quick and if a player wasn't careful he could be looking one way and the ball could literally hit him in the back of the head. It was a fast and furious game and it was played the most.

The rest of the sports, such as tennis, handball, and touch football seemed to be pretty tame compared to hoc-soc.

There was no official soccer or baseball or any such team from Kenrick Seminary that was allowed to compete in a league, but there were gentlemen who could play with the best of any team put together on the "outside" as we called it. One in particular is even in the St. Louis Soccer Hall of Fame to this day. There were some high points in the sports field. One was when a team from the seminary was pitted against the Manchester United Team from England. They were lucky enough to win, but unfortunately I believe their plane crashed some years afterward and they all died. I really don't think it was because they beat us in soccer.

I was not an exceptional soccer player but I did seem to be around when there was an important game. One game that comes to mind was in high school when I was on the varsity team. It was in a tournament. The score was tied and the end of the game was near. We had a penalty kick and of course, the one to kick it was the best scorer and forward on the team. He was the gentleman that subsequently was admitted to the Hall of Fame. He addressed the ball, kicked with all the force and might that he was capable of at that time. And...I believe at this time the ball is still traveling in orbit along with the space station.

All hearts fell along with his. As I write this, if he reads it, he is well aware of who he is and I need not mention his name. But I will continue with the hero who saved the day and applaud his ability. As play continued the ball was kicked from the backfield and bounced near the opposition's area. As it did so, our hero, who was supposed to be playing halfback, took advantage of his position on the field, which was closer than anyone else on the field, and nailed it past the goalie to score and win the game! He shall remain nameless, but in the locker room, the coach, a Mr. Robert Guelker, who was an Olympic coach and a stickler for position play, just smiled at me and said, "You were out of position, Money." This seemed to be prophetic. I am always out of position and play to a different tune as the rest of my life can attest to. Can I help it if I play and march to where and what I feel the Lord desires?

There were many ways of passing the time when not studying, even when we were supposed to be studying. All work and no play makes for a dull life. One of the primary games to be played during study hall at night was TRANSOM BALL. This game was played with a handball or at times even a tennis ball, but a handball was quieter and did not disturb the guards. Every room had a transom over the door. The door itself had panes of glass which were smoked or colored milk white. So was the transom. The transom was opened just enough to allow a ball to pass through it. The player had a certain number of shots to try and put the handball through the crack in the transom. He had to stay a certain amount of feet back and could not slam-dunk the ball. If played correctly there would be minimal sound and the floor guard – the dean, would be unaware of the sport. Anything for diversion when one is locked up.

The other diversion was a radio. If one wanted to take the chance he could smuggle in a radio. In those days there were not as many small transistors as there are now, so this could be quite chancy. I had the fortune (a gift of my father) to have a small crystal radio. It was shaped like a rocket ship and was small enough to be hidden almost anywhere and it would remain unnoticed. After lights out I would hook up the antenna wire to the water pipe of the washbasin and could bring in KMOX with Harry Fender at the Chase Park Plaza. This was heaven.

One of the most unique ways of outdoing the powers that were...the guards of the floor...was the ability to keep one's lights on after lights out. One of my classmates, who really liked to sleep during the day and stay up at night, procured some black cardboard and cut it to the size of the door, transom glass, and even the window that every room had. No light could escape out. This, of course, had to be taken down during the day to avoid detection.

There were no alcoholic beverages allowed, but who could find fault with rum balls? Talk about a cheap pseudo high! I think it was the thought that counts. At times, when grape juice was served for breakfast or even apple juice, some enterprising individual would attempt a fermentation process in his locker. I believe the smell of dirty sweat socks masked the smell of the fermenting alcohol. I had no supply problem since I was in charge of emptying the cruets of wine used at Mass. Waste not, want not. There was many a morning after Mass and before breakfast that the day did not look so bad. Being a sacristan did have its benefits even if the pay was not so good. It also kept me popular with quite a few classmates. Some chose to be more daring and hung a fishing line out the window and a friend would stop by and, in a very real sense "hook a brother up!"

Aside from sports and studying there really wasn't much else to do in the seminary, which is not unusual I guess.

Nevertheless, there were some unusual occurrences that did make the seminary different from normal college and training. It was a totally male society and except for the nuns that did the cooking, there were no women or female influences of any sort. The nuns were not allowed to fraternize with the students and because of this there was a sigh of relief from the student body. The nuns at that time were a sure cure for concupiscence. They were from Poland and could have passed for recently being freed from a German concentration camp. I am teasing, because they were a great and godly bunch of ladies and they worked from dawn to dusk. Too bad they couldn't cook that well.

There was a time when a new parish was being built in the neighborhood and until the church would be completed, services would be held in the seminary chapel. There would not normally be anything out of the ordinary about this, but don't forget, even the hall walls themselves were infused with maleness.

Then bring in a regular Sunday morning service, which in any usual parish in the St. Louis area would not cause any disruption among a normal population. But remember, this was not a normal population, and all of Sunday mornings changed. On Sunday mornings, instead of the average male walking to and from the dining room or chapel, and the normal concomitant male smells, there arose a foreign element. That element was the clatter of high heels and perfume. Even without the vision of the feminine form, that alone was enough to raise the testosterone level of the students to one that was off the scale. Everyone wanted to hang around the chapel on those Sunday mornings. At least for the first few services held in the chapel. After that, it was business as usual, almost as if the student body were at home for a typical Sunday service. The heart is not the only thing that absence makes more important. At times the seminary felt like jail or the army, and this was one of those times that really brought home that realization. Not a very normal population, but one with one goal in mind that kept it together. This was true at least most of the time.

I'm sure that this kind of attitude is foreign to those seminarians who come and go as they please today, and are allowed to be in situations where simple things are not so out of proportion. At least, I hope that this is so. I guess there are pros and cons for both sides of the question, but to keep a group of people sheltered or away in any sense, from the common situations of life, seems to make those normal situations abnormal when they are encountered. I will add that the smell of perfume has never been so sweet and so alluring as on those Sunday mornings when the services were held at our chapel. This is true except in the case of the perfume that my wife wears. It has attracted me for over forty years and continues to do so to this day. (P.S. I can be a diplomat at times.)

Reading was another activity. This I did with diligence. Most of what I read that wasn't related to studying was of a metaphysical nature or psychology oriented. Metaphysics and psychology have always interested me and the library in the seminary was filled with both subjects. I did like to read other books also.

I remember reading the RISE AND FALL OF THE THIRD REICH in three days...non-stop. I played sick and didn't even go to the dining room to eat. This was not due to interest in Germany or Adolph Hitler, but was an attempt to learn what had not been taught to me in the course of my studies. The same was true of Michener's HAWAII. I have also always been interested in English literature and novels and biographies such as Churchill's biography. These three stick in my mind because they were all read non-stop in one or two days.

I think that the seminary training was a little paranoid in some respects as to what we could read or see. The newspapers that we were allowed to read had the bra ads cut out when a department store advertised them. I really think someone had a problem but I won't make any accusations about whom it might have been. I know it wasn't me. Another time there was a big deal made about someone bringing in Mickey Spillane mystery detective books. Everyone was called into the dean's office and questioned as to whether or not they had read them.

It was real contraband. After all, we were in our twenties and these books were supposedly pornographic. That was the way it was treated. When I was asked did I read them I said no, of course not. I had read them years ago, but not while I was in the seminary. Boy, was I lucky. Those that did read them were immediately thrown out of the school. No one asked me if I had *ever* read them so I was not lying. Mental reservation. They had taught me well.

Those people who were delayed vocations had the most trouble. They had mainly been in the army or armed service and didn't understand that even though we were all men, they could not walk from the showers with only a towel. It seems that it freaked out the dean. With all the emphasis on modesty it has puzzled me why there was so much priestly abuse of children. Could it be something deeper? I think it is. I know the faculty had a big responsibility to screen out the pedophiles and perverts, but I think it failed in its efforts.

Anyway, I was reading contraband literature by Pierre Teilhard de Chardin, an excommunicated priest, biologist and metaphysician who has since been exonerated. It is a shame that I had to keep his works under my bed. After all, it could have been Playboy!

I also had played Ellie in the musical SHOWBOAT, and as I was told that I did such a good job, my name was brought up at a faculty meeting as possibly being gay. God, this was really pretty far out. Nothing came of it and I was glad. What a joke. We were all playing a game in order to get ordained. That too was a shame. It was hard to be normal under the circumstances, but we did what we had to in order to survive.

When the news of the birth control pill was circulating around it caused quite a stir. It was a real topic of moral discussion and conversation. It seemed strange to me that a person could go to hell for using the pill, no matter what the intention was for using it.

Damnation depended upon the time of the month in a moral action, but regardless, there would be damnation depending either upon a rubber or a pill for the same action. Legal mumbo jumbo is what it seemed to me. When a professor said in class that we should not condemn a person who used the pill right off the bat because we did not have to sleep next to a woman we loved, I began to think that there was some sanity somewhere, maybe even in the seminary.

The spiritual life itself was sometimes a matter of question in my mind. There was a school spiritual director that had a close connection with God. In fact, he was so old he came before God. Everyone had to go to him at least once around Lent so he could explain that fasting was not to be fun but actually a horrible experience. The more horrible it was, the better it was. You could eat almost nothing for breakfast, just a little more for lunch, and a little more for dinner. Absolutely nothing between meals. He did not understand that without peanut butter one would receive from home, we would be fasting all the time, even outside of Lent.

The crowning glory of this meeting was when he asked if we used the DISCIPLINE. Being very unspiritual I had no idea what he meant. He showed me by opening a closet door and there, lo and behold, was a cat o' nine tails hanging on the wall. He didn't push it but he didn't have a chance either. I was out of there in a New York minute shaking like a leaf for fear that I might have to use it to get ordained. It was not the case, but had it been I definitely would not have been ordained. He was not the norm, but sometimes you didn't know what the norm was. Thank God I had a reasonable and good spiritual director that had some common sense or I would not be writing this as I am today.

There was always music to listen to in the music room which had a stereo record player for use of the students only. It was here that I spent a lot of Saturday afternoons with a good friend listening to opera. Opera was not liked by most of the population, so the room was relatively available for certain on Saturday afternoons for Bill and me. Bill was about 6'4" or 5", and a bear of a man but with a soul of a wimp. (Not really, but you expected him to be rough and tough. He was not. He was a gentle giant.) After ordination we went fishing in Canada together, but that is another story. He has already passed. It was with him that I was first introduced to Puccini, Verdi, and others. Our favorite was Turandot with Luciano Pavarotti. I still get chills when I hear NESSUN DORMA. Bill was also the one who played the horses that caused me a problem, but again, it was not his fault.

Somewhere in about the second year of college, the rector of the seminary...the really big honcho...asked me in an offhanded sort of way if I would like to go to Rome. It was customary at that time to pick two students who seemed promising to travel and finish their studies in Rome. I laughed and said there was no way I wanted to go to Rome. That was for the ones who would wind up being hierarchy. It was not for me. He may have been kidding, or may have been testing me by merely running the idea by me, but my ego kicked in as it has over the years.

There was another student of Italian descent, a good student named Rico, who could be hierarchy material more than me. He also was asked if he would like to go to Rome. He was so Italian that one would have thought he would have jumped at the chance. He was from the Italian Hill section in St. Louis and he considered anyone who was not from the Hill to be, as he called them, AMERICANS. He declined. Neither of us had a desire for the Red. As far as I know, Rico and I were the only ones chosen. That year no one was sent to Rome with the excuse that our class was too rebellious. I don't know and I never will what the real reason was for not sending two students to Rome, but we were both glad that we never did have to formally decline. We were both happy to just make pizzas.

There was a pizza and spaghetti dinner for about five hundred parents and visitors for a special occasion (which now I do not remember what it was). But Rico and I smelled like pizza for days because we were the chefs who cooked the entire dinner for everyone. It was a lot of work, but also a lot of fun for we had the run of the kitchen. We both had made pizza before, but never in that quantity. What an experience.

It does seem that I was always involved in major undertakings such as putting together and managing booths for carnival days or such. I was always involved in plays from early on and was really quite a ham. I loved the applause, and as the singing and dancing "girl", Ellie, in Showboat, I really loved the standing ovation. Too bad show biz passed me by, but I know I would never have made it. Too much discipline.

The seminary was a unique experience over fifty years ago. I know it has changed today, and I think it had to be for the better in some ways. To a certain extent I don't think the majority of the students today would believe what it was like in "the good old days." It really was a tough regimen. It was like having a perpetual headache – you just got used to it.

Healing Contradiction

I am not an expert on the healing process in prayer. God is the only one who knows what is going on. I do have some questions that I need answers to and I hope He is guiding me and leading me in my mental questioning.

There are times when a prophet or one who can see the future will declare that the person will be healed physically. In one particular case I am thinking of, the prophet declared that the Lord would heal this woman of cancer. The cancer returned. Now my question is, "What happened?" She has no pain but the cancerous growth has returned even though she did what the prophet declared or urged her to do, that is to get prayer from her mother. I have inquired about this from people more versed than I in the workings of God, and they have declared that there is no answer! God will do what He desires to do and it is not dependent upon us.

Could it be that because we are spiritual beings first and foremost, that the spirit we have will be healed even though the body is not? I guess what I am trying to say is that if the reality of this life is in our spirits, then it would follow that the most important element in healing is the healing of the spirit, meaning that person may have no pain and he or she is ready to go to the other side which would indicate a healing in the real world. At times, the healing can be and often is, twofold, the healing of both body and soul or spirit. At other times, even though the prayer is for physical healing, the most important element of the healing process is the spiritual healing. God knows which is the most important part to be healed. Most certainly, even though we may be healed at one time in our lives, we are sure that we ultimately will die. Real healing leads to a change in our relationships or in our spiritual lives. Could it be that if this change in our spirit does not happen, then the healing does not last either? I don't know. We seem to judge everything in the material or physical sense and do not usually look deeper. Perhaps, we need to become more aware of the depth of our beings so that we become aware of what God really desires.

For me, this seems to be the logical reason why some people do not SEEM to be healed, but in the REALITY WHICH WE DO NOT SEE, are really healed. Only God knows for sure. It is always up to Him, for we are only present when He decides to work what we see as a miraculous healing, and when it does not happen, it is really still up to Him to know the truth as to whether or not the person is healed.

Again, it goes back to the supposition that we are first SPIRITS HAVING A HUMAN EXPERIENCE, not PHYSICAL BEINGS STRIVING FOR A SPIRITUAL EXPERIENCE.

Ordination and My First Assignment

Ordination time was nearing. It was slated for March 14th, 1964. It was to be held at the Cathedral of St. Louis. This was going to be what I had looked forward to for at least twelve years. The announcements, chalice, etc. had all been procured. There was to be a retreat before the day came. We would then climb on the bus as ordinary people and not return until we were clergy. I could hardly believe it was going to happen. I would be that bridge between Man and God, which was my whole reason (or so I believed at the time) to become a priest. Idealism was pounding through my veins.

The Cathedral was crammed with people and the smell of candles and incense. The music was beautiful. I felt as if I were in a surreal picture during the ceremony.

When asked to promise celibacy for the rest of our lives, I held back with what I had learned from my training – something called

MENTAL RESERVATION. Yes, I promise not be marry – unless I can. Maybe...just maybeeee...I cheated and I am glad to this day that I did. I was now ordained a priest according to the order of Melchisedech, whoever that was. The rest of the day was a blur; giving the first blessings as a newly ordained, the reception welcoming all the relatives and friends, and receiving gifts, etc. I was as high as a kite and reveled in the achievement of lasting through twelve years of training. This was the big time I had been waiting for all those years. After a week or so of saying Mass in other churches for people who had helped along the years, we received our first parish assignments. I was assigned to Our Lady of Providence parish, which was supposed to be an upper class new parish. The only drawback was that the pastor was a tough old liner who had an even tougher time hanging on to assistants. I thought I would be different. Wrong again... I lasted a year.

As is usually the case whether it is an ordination or a wedding, there is the day that you wake up and say; "What happened? Now this has become a job and its time to get to work. Where's the excitement?" I really didn't mind the work, and in fact loved it – visiting the sick, saying Mass, hearing confessions, working with the youth. It was all those things that I was cut out to do and enjoyed. At the same time I began to read about the new voices urging change in the church and was filled with hope of change. There were many forward-looking theologians who began to speak out without fear of recrimination. In the seminary during the latter years we were urged to try new things in the liturgy and to read with an open mind of what the Holy Spirit might bring to the Church. We were to be the vanguard generation of change. In fact, the older priests called us the "New Breed". Most of them were not happy campers, although some were more open to the changes than others.

The pastor was O.K. at first, but then when he began to train me in the way he was trained, I began to see a wall between us as how the priesthood was to be lived. My way wasn't his but I could keep my mouth shut (at least for a while) and survive his torments. At first, I did not realize his alcoholism was so pronounced until I got to know him and live with him. He did all he could, poor man, to change me but it didn't work.

He allowed me to take the census of the parish but I was not to go to certain homes. These were his people even though they did not know it. I was very well accepted as the new assistant and I believe for the most part, the people connected with me, and I with them. This he did not like. We were in a popularity contest and I didn't know it. I was just doing what I perceived to be my job and ministry. Any time that he saw me being friendly with one of HIS people he would turn himself inside out and get between us by giving me something else to do, or by belittling me as being the YOUNGSTER. It was very frustrating for me but it only got worse the longer I was there.

I was not allowed to do anything that could be looked upon as being a minister to the people if he did not sanction it. This was no different from what many of my classmates in parishes with older priests had experienced. I figured that was the way it was but it was extremely wearisome. When he was angry with me (which was quite often) he would not tell me about what, but would refuse to talk to me for several days. This made mealtime with him very painful for me. The final straw came one Sunday, when I was late helping to give out communion, because I had helped one of the nuns carry her suitcase into the convent. I was only a couple of minutes late. He did not talk to me for three days. By this time I was really fed up with this type of childish behavior and with my usual high intelligence, I proceeded to not talk to him or try to connect with him at all. This bugged the hell out of him. He couldn't take it for as long as I had! After two days he asked for a meeting with me and asked me what was wrong.

I had it penned up for so long it came out in a rush and I told him what I thought of him and his childish attitudes about everything and said I was fed up with the entire cohabitation. (Nice word.) I do not remember exactly the words I used, but I do believe that he was shocked by the way I spoke. After all, my father was a truck driver.

My priesthood had been frustrating for a year so I spoke to an older friend who had some influence with the main office and those who placed the assistants. I requested a change to another parish, which I did get in Pine Lawn. It was in a rougher neighborhood, and a changing parish, but one I had been familiar with as I grew up. The pastor had a reputation with some of the clergy, but I had not heard why he might not be liked. He loved the poor, he did not stand on formality, and he was kind to the children and compassionate to everyone who deserved compassion. He was opinionated, but so was I. We got along great! The priesthood for him was one of service and not being served, contrary to what I had experienced at my first parish. The next two years were great, and I felt almost fulfilled, but not quite.

The Reluctant Protestor

Did I mention Selma? Well, having been ordained for only a short time I wasn't really very aware of what the real world was all about. This pertained to my first pastor who had a way of not telling the truth all of the time. I found this out much later. He wasn't mean about it, but really believed since he was older and "more seasoned and the boss," he could do what he wanted with the YOUNGSTER (ME)! Coming in one night after 9 p.m., I found a note on my desk saying that the Cardinal had called and he wanted me to go to Selma, Alabama the next morning to finish the walk with Martin Luther King to Montgomery. Groups of clergy were going from St. Louis to give support for the people of Alabama in the struggle for the right to vote. Along with the note there was a pass for the plane ride that was leaving at 7 a.m. from old Lambert Field.

Although I was not a political protestor, I was somewhat aware of the struggles of the Negro population in the South and the cruelties that were visited upon them. I felt honored that the Cardinal would choose me to be part of the contingent of clergy that would be leading the fight for civil rights with Dr. King. Not to mention it would be my first plane ride! All expenses paid...what little there were. I never gave it a second thought. Tomorrow I would carry the BANNER OF JUSTICE AND HUMAN RIGHTS!!!

I was at the airport by 5 a.m. The old airport terminal was bare and stark and had only been used for, it seemed, certain occasions. There were about 50 clergy gathered together in groups. Some I knew as old seasoned priests who had been around for a while. I only saw two of my own classmates, but they were the two who really were political advocates for any cause. And this was a big one. I was getting pumped. We small-talked for a bit. The air was tense and there was an atmospheric expectation of something really big going on. To a degree my feeling was one of fear and excitement. The fear was, because I had visions of BULL CONNER and his dogs attacking helpless Negroes and Whites who stood up for the Negro. (This was seen on the nightly news and really didn't have any emotional impact on me, other than being glad that I was several hundred miles north.) It was excitement, because it would be my first plane ride...that is, until I saw the plane, and then my excitement joined my fear. It was a DC-3 and I was sure it saw many miles over the Burma Hump in WWII. Not only that, but it was owned by OZARK AIR LINES. This was not a premier airline in those days, and is now defunct. We trooped out to the plane in the dark and cold morning air and climbed into the seats. I was shocked to see how small the plane was. I had envisioned a large comfortable interior. Wrong. It really was so small that if it had mice they would be running around hump-backed! Too late to back out now... the engines were beginning to turn over and my excitement mounted as we began to trundle down the runway.

I became aware that we were traveling faster than I thought, but not fast enough to get off the ground. At least this was my impression. Then with a sigh that old DC-3 lifted herself up and we were airborne! What a thrill! The noise from the engines was deafening but they were working and for the next hour or so I really enjoyed the views from 12,000 feet. It would be about a four-hour trip. It was a clear day with scattered clouds and we weaved in and out of the puffy white balls. I was getting more comfortable all the time and really didn't care to talk much with my fellow passengers. My two classmates were on board but we did not have an opportunity to sit together. After all, we had been together for at least 8 years anyway. As I recall the landing was uneventful and I felt that flying was really great after all, even though I had seen a glider crash when I was seven years old.

We were met by a bus that had a welcoming contingent of Black men who greeted us warmly, but who wasted no time introducing us to what was to come. I remember one giant Black man with a Russian style hat who was the leader. He reminded us that we were in hostile territory, and because we were clergy, we would stand out as real troublemakers from the North and were fair game for the Alabama Cracker. We should not get separated from the group, but if we did because of violence (?) (Now the spine began to stiffen!), we were to head for the nearest Black church or seek sanctuary only from Black people. At this point I was definitely thinking that this was really foreign to me and maybe the Cardinal didn't really know what he was doing with me after all. But...too late. I was committed. The bus moved through the city of Montgomery and met up with the group that had marched from Selma. It was at this point that we joined with Dr. King and the fellow marchers who supported him, both Black and White. We were again advised not to talk to any bystanders along the March route, at any cost, as this may lead to violence and play into the hands of the Alabama Police and Militia. (Again, that nasty "V" word which caused a feeling that had been foreign to me for so many years.)

We were flanked on both sides by National Guard troops and police as the March began to pick its way through the city of Montgomery. At first I thought I would be safer with the National

Guard, but found out very quickly that this was only wishful thinking. I don't believe that the armed guardsmen were supposed to talk to us either, but as the March paused a bit, I was standing just a couple of feet away from one of them. I heard what he called me, and those who were with me, but I didn't hear it in church. I did hear it before as I rode on the truck with my father. Common language. And if that didn't hit home, the wad of spit almost did! Not looking at him I focused my gaze on the federal marshals on the rooftop and wondered whose side they were on. They were armed too, even as was my new-found friend from the guard. I was feeling very alone, to say the least. As I recall this was the only incident with me, but others had even worse, as I found out later. There were many people on their porches blessing us and thanking us for being there, but those folks didn't have guns. I felt some anger beginning to brew at the inequity of it all, not to mention the injustice. There was nothing to be done but March for support and hope for the best.

We arrived at the place where Dr. King was to speak and I can honestly say I don't remember much about it. The crowd was large and my two classmates and I had joined up. To tell the truth we were more concerned about getting back to the airport as quickly as possible because we were told that once the speech was over we were on our own in getting out of town. I do believe as good Catholics we left a little early as one does with Mass to avoid the crowds!

We made our way out of the crowd and quickly took off our collars. Now it was just a couple of guys in black suits (or so we hoped!). The fear that had been there all day was even more intense as we looked for a way to quickly get back to the airport without the "V" word. Spying an empty cab, we were very relieved when the driver said he would take us to the airport. What a relief! No "V" word this time.

Back at the airport we waited in the small terminal for the time of departure. Others from the group came in little by little but it was too soon for us to get on the plane. We just stood around nervously waiting. I was standing with my two classmates when I noticed a policeman staring at us. He could have passed for a German Storm Trooper. Maybe Gestapo. I averted his stare and looked around at almost anything. But there he was. Just waiting and staring. I remarked about this to my two friends who counseled me to not pay any attention to him. I tried to do this but when he began slapping his baton into his hand and staring straight at me something in me seemed to snap. Looking back at it, I believe my fear turned to anger. I told my two friends that I was going over to him to talk to him. By this time I was staring back. I remember him looking pleased and that angered me even more. I believe my genetic Mediterranean blood was getting the best of me. What a fool! But I didn't care. I took one step in his direction and a quick as lightning, my two classmates, one on each arm, literally almost picked me up and hustled me through the door to the plane that was now loading. I felt saved and yet cheated. My two friends knew better than to let a hot-headed "Dago", as they called me later, be so stupid. What could have happened made me ashamed of myself, as I am to this day.

As a footnote, both my classmates subsequently went to Bolivia and Chile and did do some political and spiritual work with the populace. They always had better sense than me, and I do thank them from the bottom of my heart for saving my butt from the bottom of a swamp.

I would like to say the plane ride back was uneventful, but it seemed to end as the entire day was encapsulated in that plane ride. As the plane taxied down the runway, I remember looking to the West at the sun setting behind some dark clouds and thought; "So, this is what the sunset looks like in the West when seeing it from the sky." Wrong.

They were storm clouds.

We began to run into the storm over Birmingham. It hit the plane with a vengeance. The updraft took the plane straight up as if it would never stop. Then the other hand pushed it straight down until I thought we had hit the ground. (I failed to mention that, before this, the light came on to fasten seat belts. The stewardess went into the cockpit cabin and when she came out she sat directly in front of me, a couple of seats forward. At the first updraft and downdraft her eyes became as big as saucers. This did not make me feel very good.) I will spare exposing my fear to the reader, which lasted for the next four hours. Needless to say, we were all over the sky. Up, down, wing over, rain, lightning, icing, darkened cabin, etc. If you have been through it you probably know what I mean. At one point I thought the wing was coming off because after the pilot turned on a light to check the wing, I heard a sound that could only have been rivets coming loose. In fact, it was de-icing. (Remember, dear reader, this was only my second flight, and I had seen a glider lose a wing in flight.)

Up to this time I remember saying the Act of Contrition about two thousand times just in case God didn't hear the first one. I had put my head between my legs and kissed my ass goodbye. My seatmate had done the same thing several times during the course of this flight so I felt I was doing the right thing. The difference between his action and mine was that he had a bottle which he was sipping for courage. And he didn't even offer me a sip!!!

Upon landing in St. Louis, we were told by the pilot that we could not fly over the storms and that we had to dodge at least three tornadoes. So what we endured was at approximately eight thousand feet. He apologized for the rough ride but I was glad to be on the ground. My seatmate, who was a revered monsignor, said it was the roughest flight he had ever been through, and he had been flying for twenty five years.

I had a little Volkswagen and after saying polite goodbyes, I pulled it up around my waist and ran home as quickly as my little feet would carry me.

The entire day I would never forget and prayed it would never be repeated. The final irony of the day was that I found out I was not supposed to go but that the pastor was supposed to go. I guess the Lord knew best. (P.S. I did fly again. Several times. But I have to say it isn't my favorite thing.)

Upon arriving back at the rectory, the pastor wanted to know what had happened. I told him about the entire trip. At this point I did not think it wise to tell him that I knew he was supposed to go. Silence is Golden. He was very supportive of my trip and thanked me very much. I really was happy that I had gone regardless of the fear.

I was getting back into the normal routine of the week which felt good to me. The pastor was a good man, but his ideas were from the 30's and 40's as was his theology. He'd been a Marine chaplain in the Second World War, and loved to tell war stories. I had my doubts as to the veracity of most of them, but what did I know? On Saturday before the Sunday services, he called me into his office.

He suggested in a very fatherly way, that it would be best if no one in the parish knew that I had been to Selma. It was an upper middle class parish (even had some very rich parishioners – August A. Busch was one of them) and he said he really didn't want to disturb them. In reality he was afraid that the collections would fail! I graciously acceded to his request and said I understood.

Sunday morning came and at the time for the sermon I walked from the altar to the podium to begin my talk. The first words out of my mouth were; "I JUST CAME BACK FROM SELMA, ALABAMA." I then described for the remainder of the talk how it felt to be Black in the South, and the moral responsibility that we all had for our Black brothers. He didn't talk to me for three or four days, which was standard operating procedure with him.

This parish was my first assignment and it was a tough one, as everyone in the diocese knew. I don't think they knew just how tough. Most of the previous assistant pastors asked for a change or just left the priesthood when they could.

Times were changing and there was a great deal of confusion in both theology and liturgy. And I was right in the middle of it. It was going to be a difficult task to get along with the "Old School" who would not change, and stay true to the values of the Second Vatican Council of Pope John XXIII who was the leading influence in my latter years in the seminary. Obviously, my pastor was not of what was called THE NEW BREED. I was one of the latter. The rest of the year was one of détente. If he didn't like what I did or said, he would not confront me but only stare out of the dining room window and ignore me. We really had some great meals!

In all fairness, as I look back at it, the times were really tough on the older pastors. My pastor was a little more closed to changes than normal, but basically he couldn't help it. In the later years, after I was married, I had a dream or more like a vision. I was in the rectory, the doorbell rang and he was at the door in a wheel chair. He was totally gray and did not look peaceful. He asked me would I forgive him and of course, I said yes. From that time on, any negative feelings I had for him were gone and I hope and believe that he was also at PEACE.

The Veil of Disease –

Cancer

The following are some of my ideas on cancer in general. I am not a doctor and do not have a great deal of experience with it, but I have seen enough of it to form my own opinions. We need to drop the veil that clouds our thinking on many things. Cancer is only one of them.

THE VEIL IS THE FOCUS ON THE BODY AND MATERIAL THINGS OF THIS WORLD TO THE DETRIMENT OF THE SPIRIT OF MAN.

In the mid 1930's the United States developed a product called margarine. It came in a white block of a soft substance. Along with it came a small yellow capsule that was broken into the white block and mixed thoroughly turning it the color of butter. It was to be the substitute for butter during the WWII years.

Before the marketing of this substance called margarine, a German firm was contracted to run tests upon it to determine whether or not this would be a good product as a substitute for butter. The firm did its testing and did determine that it would be a good product, but also cautioned that it might cause cancer in humans. Due to the war and for financial considerations the product was marketed in this country and around the world. There have been many additions to this vegetable oil product, most in making it taste better. Is it a coincidence that cancer has flourished for the past half century? I think not. There is no such thing as coincidence.

In my opinion, our attitude toward cancer has been one of treating the effects of the disease rather than being pro-active. I am not an M.D. but I do believe that if God didn't make it, we shouldn't eat it. I know that professional treatment specialists perform wonders in healing some cancers, but wouldn't it be better if we prevented it rather than focus on healing the effects of it?

If you follow the money trail you will find that billions of dollars are spent in the present course of cancer treatment. This is not to mention the trillions of dollars the drug companies make. Of course, it does keep our economy growing and technicians employed along with other ancillary jobs.

Think of what would happen if we all began to eat healthy instead of worrying about how we look? Would we all look like little blimps waddling around? I doubt it. Of course we may have to cut down on some calories but that would be a good thing, along with walking to the gym instead of driving. This is all probably common knowledge and I am not speaking as knowing all about cancer. But I do have some ideas on the subject that I need to express.

To my understanding cancer is a systemic cellular disease. It doesn't come upon one suddenly but comes as a disruption of cell multiplication. If we consider the fact that we are spirits having a human experience rather than humans having a spiritual experience, is it not possible that our spirit holds the answer to the healing of cancer?

Not everyone develops cancer even though screenings are advocated for everyone. Some therapies for cancer do consider the entire person, their attitudes, and outlook upon life in general. This seems to hold much promise. Some people who have died of other causes and have had autopsies are found to have had cancers which never caused them a problem. In all probability it is a combination of a healthy mind in a healthy body. I believe that we have concentrated too much upon the body to the detriment of also healing the mind. We know that one's attitude, either negative or positive, influences the healing of the cancer patient. This leads one to believe that the doctors who tell the patient that this cancer usually leads to another type of cancer are espousing a self-fulfilling prophecy. Even though they may have good intentions I feel it to be a disservice to the patient. What I am stating here is probably being done in a great many cancer treatment facilities, but I believe the general public should be more aware of what is going on. We really are seeing a better understanding of cancer treatment for the most part.

<u>Canada</u>

It was either the first year I was ordained or shortly before as a deacon that Bill, the gentle giant, and I went to Canada to go fishing. I was really excited, for this was a life-long dream coming true. He and I got along very well and we could see no problem with being together for a vacation. We drove up in Bill's new car as he had gotten ordained the year before. We drove non-stop for twenty five hours to get to Winnipeg and stayed at a place called FROSTY'S RESORT. Bill had found it by an ad in a magazine. It was set way back in the North Woods and according to Frosty himself, the walleye, pike, and bass almost jumped in the boat before you could throw a line. From his vast collection of lures, we purchased the ones that Frosty suggested – the ones that the fish would really hit on. I had gone out before we went to Canada and bought the top of the line rod and reel. I was sure to catch fish with this gear. We fished all day with Frosty the first day. (We only had three days to fish and two to travel.)

We only caught a couple of pike – not really much of what we expected in Canada. We could have done just as well in a northern state like Minnesota. Frosty assured us we would do better the next day as he had lined up a half day with another guide to fish for walleye. We went and had a great day fishing and a wonderful shore lunch of walleye and beans and sliced tomatoes. The food was the best I have ever eaten but the day and the outdoors had nothing to do with it, I am sure. I hooked a huge fish and, as usual, it got away. No kidding!

When we got back to Frosty's he told us that there was a virgin lake about a mile through the woods where the fishing was tremendous. The boat we could use would be sunk, but we could bail it out and all would go well. He hoped we were strong enough to carry all the fish home. The mile walk would not have been so bad if it were not for the army worms. Anyone who has walked a mile in the Canadian brush knows what I am saying, but if you add ten million army worms (caterpillars) who love to crawl on human skin and down your back you have got a mix straight from hell. It was also just as warm. Sure enough, Frosty was right. The boat was sunk and it took a bit to raise. We began to fish. I had been having trouble with my wonderful expensive rod and reel and today was the worst of all. I had about 65 yards of line in the bottom of the boat when we came around a small island. As we rounded the island, the DEVIL OF FISHING LINE took off with all 65 yards. It was a mass of twisted nothing that could be used. I invented a few words, and we both decided that this was not the virgin lake for us and we headed back to the wonderful resort area through the brush and another ten million army worms! Frosty was very apologetic but promised a great trip that evening on the Winnipeg River, and he would be our guide. In the meantime, I threw my entire rod and reel in the lake and purchased a new, cheaper one.

That evening was beautiful. The weather had cooled and we would have about four hours to fish because the sun did not set until about 10 p.m. Bill and I were really excited considering the virgin lake incident. It made me doubt there was ever such a thing as a real virgin.

Forgive me, Mother of Jesus, but the evidence is only hearsay, especially among fishermen.

Well, to make a long story short, we didn't catch one fish. Nada. We were leaving the next day or thereabouts (the fishing stunk, but as Frosty said, "We should have been there last month.") and I could have killed there and then. But even more because of what followed on the way back to the resort. We were traveling up the middle of the Winnipeg River when we heard sirens going off. Since this was downstream from the Winnipeg dam and locks it meant that they were opening some of the locks as Mr. Frosty explained. Bill and I naturally assumed since he was an experienced guide in this part of Canada, he would know what to do. After all, he had even pointed out the Hudson Bay's first outpost along the shore as we fished. I could see the white water rushing at us over Bill's looming hulk. He was in the front of the boat, I in the middle, and Frosty at the helm, running the outboard motor.

It was when the first wave hit and Bill disappeared below the water with me close behind that I began to think we may be in trouble. I mean BIG TROUBLE! The second wave did not seem much smaller, and it swallowed up Bill and me for the second time. This was it. We could not sustain another wave like the first two. Thank God we didn't have to. The third wave would have pushed over the Titanic but it was worn out before it hit us. The boat was foundering and filling with water quickly. All our gear was lost, including my father's movie camera that I had borrowed for the momentous trip of a lifetime! I turned to look at Frosty who had been wearing a panama hat which was now plastered to his head. His eyes were huge and he was screaming loud enough to be heard in Toronto. "BAIL, BAIL, BAIL, BAIL." He was also shaking like a leaf, but he was finally steering the boat as well as he could toward the shore. We made it to the shallows and pulled the boat and ourselves to land. We had decided that Mr. Frosty was a dork but we didn't know how much of a dork he was. When we asked why he didn't head for shore at the first siren he blithely explained that he had only been up here for a couple of months. He had bought the place to get out of cab driving in New York.

Bill and I argued that night about who would get to kill Mr. Frosty first. We decided to leave before we actually did it. However, the next day gave me another experience that I could have done without.

We were again driving non-stop to get back to St. Louis which was a real twenty five hours away. The drive was through Minnesota and Iowa, as I remember. Iowa will always be with me. It was about 11p.m. when we were going through the state and I was driving. Bill was sleeping next to me and I was really pushing it. I wasn't sure what the speed limit was, but I assumed it was seventy mph. Wrong, guess again. It was, until we hit the town of Ottumwa where both city limit signs were posted on one pole. I was about two miles out of town when I saw the red lights in the rear view mirror. I pulled over somewhat puzzled, but the officer was very nice. He asked where we were from, what we had been doing, and did we catch any fish. And oh, "You are clergy, huh?" Well, he really liked the St. Louis Cardinals and listened to them all of the time when he could. He was really sorry we didn't catch any fish, "But could you please follow me back to town?" We were speeding and he was sure the judge, being a very nice and understanding person, would like to talk to us. As I pulled around to follow him, Bill asked if I had seen his car or anything unfamiliar. No, I remarked, only a camera on the side of the road, which I thought was a surveyor's equipment left over night. Well, Bill smiled. All that he said was "You were driving." Thanks, I needed that.

We arrived back at the town of Ottumwa and pulled up to a classic white house with a white picket fence, which is probably standard for all towns in Iowa. At least it was in "Music Man." We got out of the car and were greeted by an elderly gentleman in a bathrobe. He warmly welcomed us in. Oh man, I thought, I think grandpa may like me. I was sure of it when he offered me some popcorn. His daughter was making some in the kitchen and he was kind enough to consider us.

We then sat down to business. After hearing the particulars from the gendarme who busted me, he merely asked how much money I had. I figured after he found out I only had $14.50 he would certainly have pity on this poor, new clergyman. Wrong again. I believe he was a Baptist, but he did leave me fifty cents! Bill just sat there smiling. I didn't even eat his popcorn. I only hope the $14.00 was not enough to pay for the policeman's evening salary. But he probably was the judge's son-in-law and they would split the take. All this time during the entire ordeal, Bill just sat there and grinned as he'd done before.

One winter Bill and I went on a hunting trip in northern Missouri. On the way home we realized that we were considerably over the limit for rabbits. I mentioned this to Bill, and he replied that he wasn't worried because he had borrowed a gun from me. I replied that it didn't make any difference, you were only allowed so many with your license. He said he didn't even have a license so I was the only one hunting. He really was quite a good friend and I miss him, although I do think his sense of humor left a lot to be desired.

The Healing of Cancer

About six months ago I received a call from a former client requesting prayer. She was diagnosed with uterine cancer and needed an operation removing her uterus. After the operation it was discovered that her lymph nodes had cancer and she needed chemo and radiation therapy. She requested prayers after the operation. At the first prayer session she had an image of a flock of birds carrying a blanket of healing. This blanket was pulled through her body and she felt that it was possibly a healing but she was not sure. At this time she felt a great deal of peace and calm.

During subsequent prayer sessions, which took place on a weekly basis for the most part, she felt very peaceful. Images occurred to her of geese flying in a V formation and that signified to her that she was experiencing victory in her healing.

There was no prompting on my part at any time. During one of these sessions she saw Jesus clothed in a robe that had V's all over it. She began to feel that she was definitely being healed. After the first treatment of chemotherapy she was to take radiation. There was no sign of cancer at this time. She asked whether or not she should continue with radiation since there was no sign of the cancer. I would not suggest anything but during the prayer session at this time she saw Jesus and he told her she should continue with the radiation. She did continue.

Prayers continued during the radiation and also at the second round of chemo, which was prescribed by the doctors. After the second round of chemo she was declared cancer free and the treatments ended. On the day that this happened as she arrived home, she noticed a flock of geese flying in a V formation directly over her and her home as she entered it. She had never noticed geese flying in this formation prior to this time. At this writing she has no sign of cancer and has claimed a healing.

The point which seems important to me is that even though the treatment may have been responsible for her healing, she felt as she was going through the treatments that she was being healed. It makes no difference how the healing took place; the fact of the matter is that she felt the Lord was healing her. He does work in medicine also, not only in miraculous manners.

The Next Parish

My next two years at the Pine Lawn parish were very fulfilling and somewhat busy. At last I was feeling that I was a priest. The pastor let me do what I felt. I was a chaplain for the local nursing home, a periodic chaplain for the Army Reserve, along with monthly communion calls for the homebound parishioners. I visited the hospitals to see the sick parishioners and in general was pretty much acting in the capacity of a normal assistant in an active parish.

The experiences that I had at this time were pretty normal, but several were more memorable than the ordinary. At the previous parish, the pastor had taken me on a suicide call to familiarize me with the procedures on attending to the suicide victim by being the first on the scene. He was training me on the realities that would be necessary to fulfill priestly duties and for that I was thankful. He made me touch the now-cold body to become familiar with it. It was a little disconcerting but not traumatic. While I was in Pine Lawn there were two events which were a little out of the ordinary.

The first incident happened as I visited St. Mary's hospital to see someone who had pneumonia, just a routine pastoral visit. As I exited the elevator a nun was coming out of a room as a nurse was putting up a screen in the doorway. The nun grabbed me by the arm and declared, "We need you, Father!" My first inclination was that someone was passing away and I would be administering the last rites. Well, I was correct in one way, but not in the circumstances I had envisioned. On the floor lay an elder gentleman who was bleeding profusely from his neck. Blood was everywhere; walls – ceiling – mirror. The nurse was trying to get him onto the bed and asked for my help. Between the both of us we got him onto the bed and she applied a tourniquet with a towel. It would do no good and we both knew it. I began to say the prayers for the last rite (I did have my book with me). It did no good. I could neither find the page nor had enough composure to remember the prayers. The final gasps were coming from the victim, so at least realizing that time was up, I absolved him of everything possible. At that point some orderlies or others arrived and took over.

The nun and nurse thanked me, and as I began to leave they offered to help me clean up. It was at that point that I realized my shoes and pants were very bloody. Being very outwardly cool during this whole event, I accepted their offer and left the hospital looking pretty normal. No one seemed to know that I really was shook up and was feeling very guilty that I couldn't remember the last rite prayers. (I doubt if anyone could have except an old pro, which I was not. But at least I didn't faint or pass out and felt that I weathered the event pretty well.) That was until I stopped by my mother's home to clean up a little more and she offered me lunch, which I accepted. It was tomato soup. That is when I lost it, told Mom that I think I had the flu and retired to the bathroom. It was quite a day. One I will carry till my dying day.

The second memorable event at this time was a bit more humorous. We were preparing for Confirmations, which was a big event. The Cardinal was coming to perform the service and there would be a small meal and gathering of clergy afterward. This would be the first time that I would really have a chance to see the Cardinal since ordination day. After all, he did send me to Selma. About thirty minutes before he was to arrive, we got a call that a woman was in her home and had not been seen for three days. The police had been called and someone requested the presence of a priest. Since I was the low man on the totem pole, I was elected. I would be back in time for at least part of the ceremony and grab a bite to eat with the Cardinal, sucking up a little.

I arrived at the home which was surrounded by several police cars. I was told that we were waiting for the coroner to arrive because no one could break in without him. We waited and waited and waited...I could see my chances of getting back in time dwindling with each passing minute.

There was an air of jocularity among the police and they didn't seem too concerned about getting in the house. My thoughts were to break in right away, the heck with procedure. I saw what was happening later, but I was too inexperienced to realize it at the time. I found out soon enough when the coroner did arrive.

The basement door was broken into and two policemen went up the stairs to the main floor. They stopped when they arrived at the top of the stairs and called to me to come up. I hurried up the stairs and when I reached the top of the stairs and entered the house, it hit me. The smell was horrible, something I had not experienced before. She had been dead for three days. By the looks and smiles on the two cops, I knew what their little joke was. Again, they suspected what I had not. Telling them there was nothing I could do, I left. When I got to the rectory the party was over and no one was around. I gave my report to the pastor and went to bed. It was again another unforgettable experience.

Another interesting experience was with an acquaintance who worked as a policeman part time. After Saturday confessions he would pick me up and I would ride with him until the end of his watch. This was really fun for me. The thrill of a screaming siren racing to a trouble situation was a real rush. I'm sure it wasn't the same for him, but a steady job doing the same thing all the time is never too thrilling no matter what it is. I remember one incident in particular apart from issuing tickets for speeding, etc.

It was Saturday night and there was a domestic disturbance call. This was my first introduction to police procedure. You never rush to answer the call... if you got there too soon, those involved, usually the husband and wife, could have already made up and the police would be the intruders.

As intruders, the police may have to take on both the husband and wife at the same time. Not good. I saw this in actuality on the first domestic call I witnessed. We arrived at the residence in question and Tim told me to stay in the car until he called for me. He walked up the steps to the brick single residence and knocked on the door. The door opened and a short man built like a proverbial brick stepped out with an axe, which he promptly swung at Tim who was skillfully ducking using some moves I was sure he learned at the police academy. This forced the midget concrete block back into the house where great screams, breaking glass, and much cursing was emitting. (I guess Concrete Block could talk and curse!) But only for a minute! Suddenly all was quiet. I wasn't sure who survived until Tim appeared and motioned for me to come in. Concrete Block was sitting on the sofa with a bloody nose. He was handcuffed. His darling wife was on the other side of the room bewailing the fact that Tim had hit him, and was also being rude to her in making her keep her distance. When she saw me she became quiet and docile.

I don't remember if they were parishioners or not but it didn't matter. I had only seen more gin and vodka bottles at the local liquor store than there were on the table. Every one was emptied except one, and I surmised that was the villain that did Concrete Block and his bride in. By this time back-up was called and had arrived on the scene. Since our watch was over it was decided that the back-up would do the honors of taking Concrete Block to County Jail. Concrete was very docile after his tussle with Tim. It was probably the gin and vodka plus the bloody nose that made him that way. Back-up was cautioned that he had been a handful to manage a few minutes ago, and that he should remain cuffed in the car. Back-up declined. This was a mistake. Five minutes after we left, the call came in that an officer needed assistance. Seems like Concrete Block woke up and kicked in the screen between the back and front seats. Oh, well.

While I was at St. Paul's I was a Chaplin several times for the Army Reserve. This was enjoyable and something I had not experienced under the former pastor. I would say Mass for the troops on Sunday morning, performing a service for which I did not believe there would be any compensation. I found out at the end of the service that it was mandated that they take up a collection for the minister. I declined to accept it thinking that it was not necessary. They protested that it was mandatory and I went home weighted down with around seventy dollars in change. I offered it to the pastor and he promptly told me it was mine. This was really foreign to me, because the former pastor I had would not have allowed me to keep it. I was impressed and waited eagerly for the next Army Reserve meeting. There were not enough of them as far as I was concerned! One hundred dollars a month was not very much in those days, and that was my salary.

<u>Leaving</u>

It was during the first two years after ordination that I began to get in touch with what I would call the archaic laws of the Roman Church. I was allowed to think for myself and my thinking was changing me to be a liberal. There was no one to stop me. Besides, many other young priests were thinking the same way.

Enter Jackie O'Toole, a recent college graduate now teaching in our parish school of religion who was as forward thinking as me and who was to enter the convent. We thought alike and as the Lord would have it, we fell in love. We wanted to get married. Sounds simple, doesn't it? Nothing could be further from the truth. During this time I sought counsel from older priests who had the same problem. There was no help there. One person went so far as to say, "You needn't buy a cow to get milk through the fence." This was said laughingly but the general advice was to wait until the law changed. Until then, interpret the law of celibacy in the strictest sense.

You cannot marry but you can always date or make her your housekeeper. This would mean that I would be living a lie. I could not do it.

My present pastor was very kind even though his demeanor was a little rough. I understood him and he understood me. He was like a father to me and we got along well. He didn't stand on a lot of phony formality. Even though he seemed a little harsh when he found out that I was thinking about leaving the priesthood, I knew he didn't know exactly what to do. At the time I was hurt, but when I saw him several years later with my children and he was so kind to them, my wife and me, I knew I was right about his real compassion and kindness.

Gossip flies around every group of humans and the priesthood was probably the most gossipy group I had encountered. Same as the seminary. It was a Friday afternoon when the pastor knocked on my door at the rectory and asked if he could speak with me. He had heard that I planned on leaving to get married and I said that it was true. He said he didn't want anyone in his church that thought that way and felt I should leave right away. I explained that I had already talked with the Cardinal and it was determined that as long as I would not make a public announcement, he would allow me to not be included in the next reassignment, and I would just fade away into the woodwork. I thought this would take care of it and the Cardinal and I were peaceful with it. Now here was a monkey wrench in the process!

My Mediterranean genetics kicked in and I asked if it was all right if I left by three o'clock that afternoon. It was then 1:30 p.m. He agreed. I then asked if I could pick up the rest of my gear that I could not cram into my little VW on the next day. He agreed to this also. He then gave me $100 for the month which was due me, and then gave me another $100 (I think this was severance pay). I packed the car with my most treasured possessions – my guns and fishing equipment, went to the local bank, cleared out my account which consisted of $247 and change, and stopped by Jackie's apartment.

I asked her if she wanted to get married, and although she was confused as to the timing, (We did not plan this type of hurried wedding or any type for that matter.) she said yes. I said how about in three weeks? She said O.K. I headed for my folk's home, told them what had happened, and moved in with them for the next three weeks. It was probably hell for them and I didn't care. It was time for action and I was not only the soup, I was the main course as far as I was concerned.

I had a very good friend who was a pharmacist and he had connected me with someone who needed a salesman to rack GE light bulbs. I had told him I would take the job a few weeks earlier and he promised me he would wait for me. I started the following week working in the real world. Of course, when the word got around as to what happened, rumors began to fly: I was selling light bulbs and brooms much as the disabled did, and that I had to leave because of a pregnant woman, etc. Nothing could have been farther from the truth. I really was hurt, but as far as I was concerned, I was in for my life and that of my wife-to-be and there would be no backing out. Whatever would come, even though I might not be prepared for it, I would take it on.

Dick & Jackie

Wedding Day

March 29, 1967

Jackie and I were married the twenty ninth of March by an Episcopal priest, which was around three weeks after my leaving St. Paul's in Pine Lawn. I was so shook that I cannot remember the ceremony, but so much had happened I am surprised I could remember anything at all. After a three-day honeymoon I began my job as a distributor salesman for General Electric. Jackie's father had graciously given us a reception after the wedding and there were many supportive people in attendance. The minister held the marriage license for thirty days, but word had gotten out about what I had done and the city hall had been watched. The day that it was recorded it hit the newspapers and from then on, for several weeks, the media was after us. This caused my mother great pain. She was being hounded by the lead anchor on the NBC channel so much so that we changed her phone number. The holy men would not even talk to her because of what I had done. My, my, my – not all the Pharisees lived in Jesus' day. Some still live today. She was not into the fight as I was and I was sorry about that but there was nothing I could do for her. I know she suffered much, and in later years, all was not only forgiven but blessed by her. I know it was very difficult for both the families to endure the shame that we had brought upon them, but I knew then, as I know now, that it had to be a part of my life…and Jackie's too.

I'm pretty sure that on the surface we may have looked like it did not bother us to have all that attention, but in reality it was extremely painful for us both. I was doing what I never dreamed I would or want to do, but it was really done out of love for each other, and out of love for God and the changes in the Church that we thought needed to happen.

On the day that the newspapers reported what I had done, I walked into a drug store that was owned by my pharmacist friend. He yelled across the entire store, "Hey Father, you made the news!" There went my blending into the woodwork. Jackie was teaching at Parkway High School and her students wanted to know if I had robbed a gas station.

Amazing gossip also declared that I had married Sister Jacqueline Grennan, the President of Webster College, and that she was pregnant. That poor nun. There was much more that I didn't know at the time and I am glad I didn't know. I knew that I was angry, but I put that on hold until years later when I got in touch with it and grieved over it. My job now was to make a living for my wife and me.

In all fairness, I must say that what happened in 1967 and a few years before was the product of a different time and mindset. Some things have changed; some have not. But I feel that more change is on the way. I know it is for Jackie and me. I really do not have any rancor or animosity for those who I felt hated us for doing what we knew we were to do. That was forty five years ago...things have changed and change is very difficult for all humans.

Much went on the first years of our lives together. We had our Firstborn, Richard, and Great Grandma O'Toole counted the months out on her fingers in front of us and declared that it was O.K. We knew it was but I don't think very many others gave us the benefit of the doubt.

Although I had a lot to learn about lighting sales and retail selling to drugstores and grocery stores, I picked it up pretty well. In three years I was the highest paid salesman in the company, which was not good. The company was going under and guess who was the first salesman that had to go. You guessed it. Yours truly. Now what?

It was not long after I was let go from the distributor sales job that the company was bought out by Adolphus Busch Orthwein. He reorganized the company and offered me my old job for the same amount that I had been making. But the stock market was a place that some people said I was cut out to be in and where the money was big. That was for me. I passed the Securities and Exchange test with help from two or more people who walked me through it with much difficulty. But I finally made it. I was a stockbroker. Now I had status. No light bulbs for me. This was my door to big money, or so I was told. It didn't take long for me to find out that I was not cut out for being a broker. Big money, yes; Stockbroker, no. We were beginning to go under and I knew it.

It was then that Mr. Orthwein's offer came back to me. I knew the lighting retail business and he still wanted me back to work for him. I met with him and accepted his offer. He said (He knew I was in a tight spot.) that the offer was for two thousand dollars less than the original offer. I felt very angry but realizing that he had me, I accepted for the lower amount. Within three years I was General Manager and Sales Manager, and the original amount he had offered was given me. When I went with the company originally it was doing around $76,000 annually. When I left it three years later it was doing over one million annually. I knew I was doing a good job and when I asked for a decent raise, he declined. I quit and went to another distributor, which was a mistake. They used me for my information and then fired me. I was not a happy camper. The next eighteen months were a trip to hell for me. We had two boys and another baby on the way. During this time I had approximately nine different jobs, everything from concrete laborer to working in a garden nursery. Jackie was baking party cakes and babysitting to help financially. It was a very tough time for us.

I told her when we married that I would do whatever it took to make a living for us because almost everyone had said I didn't have enough training to work in the world. The one thing that I said I would NOT do was clean toilets.

An old acquaintance had heard that I was looking for a job and contacted me with an offer to work for him. He had a commercial cleaning company and offered me a job with pay close to what I had been making as a salesman. I jumped at it because at the time I was dispatching trucks for Spector Freight Trucking Company. It was three days on and three days off. The days were twelve hours each, starting at 3 a.m. to 3 p.m. My goal was to get on as an over-the-road driver. My father told me never to drive a truck. What did he know? I needed the money. But as usual he was right. Guess what? When I took the job with the commercial cleaning company the first work order was to clean the toilets at the Texaco station on Jefferson and Highway 44. I didn't give it a second thought. Talk about being humbled!!!

The job paid well, but it was long days and weekends and it kept me from my family which is not what I wanted. I left the priesthood to have a family and this job did not cut it.

The end came when I was cleaning a swimming pool with a high-pressure hose and muriatic acid. The boss didn't think I was doing a good job, and took over for me. Since I had no goggles or gloves and was getting tired of the burning spray, and he could do a better job, I quit there and then. He called a few days later and asked me to come back. I believe the job is still where the sun doesn't shine.

How to Cure A Cold

I have had an upper respiratory infection since the middle of November 2010. Today is January 23, 2011. This is the first day since November that I am not gagging and coughing. I have taken an antibiotic and followed the doctor's orders and nothing seemed to work. It was very uncomfortable and did not allow me regular sleep as I had to sit up to allow sinus drainage. I received prayer for healing of it, and was even told that it might be psychological. Nothing seemed to resonate with me as to the cause. I don't normally hear voices but a week or so ago I seemed to hear a voice saying, "I'm not going to leave you alone." I thought I really may be crazy or I made it up.

What did keep coming to me though, and my wife gave it some credibility, was that this could be an attack from our LOW ENERGY SPIRIT...commonly known as the DEVIL.

At first thought, I discounted it because we all know as humans we are susceptible to sickness. That's why we have doctors. Well the doctor didn't know what to do or what it was... it could be a new virus that will leave when it is ready. But wait a minute. God did not make us to get sick. That only happens when mankind gets hooked up with choices about Good or Evil. Sickness and disease came and still come from Evil. This can BE even though we are not aware of it. We call it just Human Nature. In looking deeper, since the Devil's job is to make us uncomfortable, sick, depressed, anxious, and anything else that is disturbing to us, why wouldn't he be happy if I would be uncomfortable for several months and make those around me distressed about my situation? How then, was I to counteract this disturbance which I then assumed was from the Devil?

If this cough and sinusitis was from the Devil and it was making him happy every time I coughed and gagged (which was frequently) what could I do to make him go away?

Obviously, if it made him happy, what was there that made him sad or cause him to beat a hasty retreat? It dawned on me that the name of Jesus would not make him happy. Moreover, if I THANKED Jesus every time I coughed or swallowed mucus he would be doubly upset and go back to tending the fires of hell or whatever. He can't stand the LIGHT OF THE UNIVERSE.

Sooooo...for the past 24 hours every time I coughed or swallowed I said loudly...THANK YOU JESUS!!! And meant it. This morning, for the first time in two months, I did not wake up coughing or gagging. Did the virus (?) run its course? Did the fires of hell become hotter because a LOW ENERGY SPIRIT was added to the mix? A coincidence? (Which I do not believe in and no thinking person would consider in any case.) I leave the conclusion up to you. Try it next time when a situation arises. It's like chicken soup – SO WHAT COULD IT HOIT!!!

Jackie and Me

I met Jackie the first year of my assignment at Our Lady of Providence. She was enrolled at Webster College at the time and not only was a daily Mass attendant, but also was very interested and conversant about the NEW CHURCH that was beginning to be thought of as a necessity for continued existence. Looking back on it I must say it was probably love at first sight. I definitely was not looking for any female companionship, but I do remember almost every detail of her dress, eyes, and smile as she walked across the parking lot where she was going to teach school. (These were not the only features that I remember either.) The exiting assistant pastor introduced her to me and that was the last I saw of her for over three months as she studied in Mexico to get her degree in Spanish as a teacher.

When I next saw Jackie she was in the church parking lot with her favorite dog, Snooper. We talked for a bit about what she was doing and going to do. That was when she asked me to be her spiritual director, because she was going to enter the convent of the Sisters of Loretto. At first I declined, saying that I was too young for such a task, but she countered with the fact that her minor at Webster College was Theology and she wanted someone who was interested in all the exciting changes happening in the Catholic Church because of the Vatican II Council. I relented and we met often.

With the new "open door" policy in the Catholic Church Jackie, another parishioner, and I represented Our Lady of Providence at Ecumenical meetings at various churches of other religious denominations. She also joined the Young Adults Club and helped with the high school group. Our Friendship began to grow, not romantically, but as one with whom I could talk to other than my statuesque pastor.

Our friendship and communication really began to blossom when it became time for her to go off to the convent. She had always wanted to be a nun and had decided to join the Order of the Sisters of Loretto several months before, and now that was time, she began to have her doubts about the life style itself.

By this time, I too had found that we could probably be closer than we were, and it scared us both. Since it had already been decided, she wanted to give it a try and she left and entered the Order as a Postulant. At the time I was at St. Paul Parish in Pine Lawn and I gave myself to my work in the parish. To a degree it was satisfying but there was something missing. In truth, there was always something missing in my priesthood. It seemed empty and superficial. I knew that I was doing good priestly work, but the work did not seem that important. Don't misunderstand – bringing the Lord to people was satisfying but it seemed there should have been more. Connections were made on the surface with people and, apart from the confessional, there was no way that I felt able to touch people's lives. On the surface it seemed fine, but inside of me it felt hollow. I know this was my personal problem and I am not blaming the priesthood or anyone else for my inadequacy. To make matters worse, I had it good at the parish.

I had a pastor I could relate to, one who was a real man and spiritual at the same time. He had a sense of humor and love for the poor and children. He was strong in his beliefs and was not hypocritical about them. As far as I was concerned, I could do as I wanted as long as it was in bounds. It always was. No matter what I was doing in the parish, I still had more time than I knew what to do with. I could leave at anytime for a day or even more if I wanted to, but everything I did was on my own.

I could only fish and hunt and play golf, (which I didn't like) so much and then I would be bored. I took up painting and loved it, but never became very good. It was good therapy however. Mostly, no matter where I was or what I was doing, I was struggling with my lifestyle. I really wanted to get married and Jackie was the girl. But here the problem really began. I also wanted to be a priest. I doubt if very many can know the pain involved in making such a decision except for the thousands who were ordained and would still be ordained and working if they could have been married also. In the Sixties it was a new problem that needed to be solved and no one in the church hierarchy seemed to really care. There was a lot of talk, but no actions really taken. It was new territory with no definite boundary or solution. It seemed that the priests were on their own in solving this problem. And they did solve it on their own, some sooner than others. I solved mine sooner. I finally decided that I was not meant to be single or celibate. A family was foremost in my thinking since realizing that the priesthood could be operational and still have a focus on the family. Most other religions allowed it and no matter what the Catholic Church said about it, as a law it was not practical or even Christ-like in my mind.

My mind was made up. Now the problem was how to go about getting married. As Jackie was still in the convent I decided to break the news gently to my mother. I announced to her one afternoon that if

Jackie came out of the convent I would marry her. Looking for a way to kill an Italian Catholic mother with an only son who was a priest? Call me.

At the announcement of this event to be, mother grabbed her chest and wanted to know why I wanted to kill her. I told her I did not. But she didn't believe me. Her shame would be so great no son would ever go through with it if he really loved his mother. I assured her of my love but would not back down on my resolve. After all, why did I have to be the first one in St. Louis (that she knew of) to do such a heinous crime? It would be many years before mother would come to grips with my decision. She tried but it was difficult for her.

To her credit, mom and Jackie became very close over the years, so much so that she loved her as a daughter. And Jackie not only felt a mother's love from mom but also was close to her on a spiritual level.

When I received a call from Jackie that the convent wasn't for her I was elated and, at the same time, fearful. She was coming home and I knew why. This was it. The die was cast and I knew it. I had to talk to the Cardinal. But when? Wait a bit and let things settle down with my family and then also with Jackie's. This was not an easy and fun-filled situation as most weddings should be. When she came home she secured a position teaching Spanish at the Parkway School District, got her own apartment and a small car and we began to date. This was not very easy and normal. First of all, I had not dated before. I hadn't even had a girlfriend in the regular sense of the word. HA! I learned, difficult as it was.

I had an older friend who had known me as a child and who shared my dream of what the Priesthood should be. He and his girlfriend took Jackie and me out and made it as normal as could be as two couples dating. Inevitably, when Jackie and I went out for dinner or lunch or almost every time we were together, we seemed to bump into either some friends or parishioners. It didn't seem to matter how far away from either parish or from the city for that matter, there was always someone there that we didn't want to see. This was not an average dating situation. Even when going to the show it seemed like everyone we knew would show up.

What did make it more normal was that the other assistant priest at St. Paul's was doing the same thing. This made it a lot easier to go out together. The momentum was building. Another classmate of mine was also doing the same thing as Jackie and I, and had the same plans.

He and I were on retreat and taking a walk when he announced that he also was finished with the priesthood and was going to take off as soon as possible with his intended. After comparing notes and consulting as to what would be the best way of handling the situation, it was decided that we would keep our cool and leave at the same time, probably in the spring. Since it was the fall it would give us time to get jobs and start to think like men getting married instead of men who had to elope. We also agreed that we would stay in town, not out of rebellion, but because it would not be right to run from something that was not even wrong. Face it and get it over with is the way I have always thought. This was my theory in action and as a theory it was great – as an action it sucked! We took static from everyone who knew what we were going to do and the number was growing rapidly. The only one that didn't know was the Cardinal. So I decided in February to tell him my plans for the future.

I made an appointment to see him about the second or third week in February and I was really scared. Fear and trepidation really cannot be expressed adequately. We met in his study and I'm sure he didn't know how filled with fear I was at the time. I told him that I didn't feel that I was cut out for celibacy and had decided that I wanted to leave the priesthood. He was very gracious. To this day I wish I could have taped the conversation. He said he understood and since he was on the commission in Rome on celibacy he declared that it was the "little Dagos in Rome that were holding it back". I could have kissed him there and then. We discussed the non-sinfulness of my actions. We both agreed there was no sin connected with it. He asked if I needed any money, and like a fool I said no. We then agreed that the best thing to do would be to not reassign me in the early summer and I would fade away into the woodwork. As long as I would not make a public issue of it, he and I both would be very happy. I left in March and he died in June. I'm sorry that he took it so hard. I didn't mean to kill him.

The Work of the Healer

The work of the healer is an evolutionary process. By that I mean that he must have an understanding of evil, sin, affliction and the love of God. Inherent in all mankind is the element of evil. This is a result of the mortality of mankind. It is not wrong, but a natural order of mortality on this planet. We may say that evil is a product of being human. We have come to look upon evil as being the same as being sinful, which I don't believe is the same thing. A person is sinful when he or she chooses to willfully partake of an act whereby they know it is wrong in the eyes of God and against the will of the Father. Affliction is the act or acts of suffering that a person endures even though they seem to not have any reason for existence. They have done nothing personally to be afflicted with any disease and yet it happens to them no matter how good they are. In all of this the only real personal act, which is against the will of the Father, is sin. This is because sin is a personal choice of the person to choose that which they know is against the Father's will. The other two elements, evil and affliction, are a part of mankind's existence upon this earth. This would explain to a degree why some good people of this world suffer afflictions, and why the so-called bad people at times prosper and have material wealth.

The love of God is present in all three elements. He does not condemn the evil in man, but rather understands that it cannot be helped as long as we are on this earth. It is looked upon as a fault rather than as a choice. Sin on the other hand is a choice and is not desired by God. Man must choose differently in order to be one with the will of the Father. This is the personal aspect of sin, and one that only the sinner can change. Affliction of the person is more or less a correction of the person's attitude that may or may not be needed. By that, I mean that affliction can also be a part of time and the events of this world, which again are not personal to the person being afflicted. In affliction the love of God is very present, but the reason for the affliction may not be understood at the time. In both evil and affliction, the love of God is always present and His peace can be had and be a supportive factor to the person. Peace of the Lord, or the grace of God, can be present to the afflicted one. There is no punishment due. Nor is punishment of the Lord due for evil in men. It is different with the sinful person because his choice, by very necessity of this choice, separates him from God. The result is pain in this world, either physical or emotional, or psychological in his spirit or soul. We have been made by God in His image and likeness and any other choice, which would separate us from His intention, is a hell of itself.

The intent of the healer, then, is to bring peace and understanding to the individual being healed so that he may see the love of God always with him no matter what the circumstances of his life. If he has chosen sin it must be renounced. If he feels that he is evil it must be understood that this is a false belief but part of his nature that must be released by a choice of desiring the kingdom of God. If he is afflicted he must understand also that this is an evolutionary process that can bring him closer to God, and can be a gift from God for his evolutionary growth leading to the kingdom. In both evil and affliction, God is present.

The love of God is not withheld from the sinner because He is always present to him. But the heart of the sinner must change for the love of God to be, as it were, activated. It is like a cell phone. You must turn it on and dial the right number before your party can be reached. The sinner must personally choose to receive the love of God and then that love will be present. Along with the choosing of God and living with the will of the Father, there is no guarantee that material wealth will come to the person. Material wealth is just that...material. Healing is of the soul or spirit and this does not necessarily mean that material wealth will follow in this world. What it does mean is that the spirit or soul of the person will find that peace which will come in only doing what the will of God desires. What is more important to all men is that deep within their hearts there is a need for that peace which only God can bestow.

It is part of our human nature and no amount of worldly treasures can make up for it. We often strive for the material, thinking that this will give us peace, only to find that even more material is needed and it still does not satisfy the longing of the heart.

I have said that healing is evolutionary, because on a worldly scale, mankind is evolving also. We are moving in all ways in an upward direction trying to get closer to the Father. It really is how we are made and what we really desire. There are many instances of the upward process although it is not immediately apparent. If we consider the growth of technology, theological awareness, and the alignment of thought throughout the world, we can become more aware of an evolution taking place. The evolution of mankind begins with each individual man, and as each individual becomes more a part of the will of God, and chooses His will, the entire human race will also evolve.

Salvation is personal and not brought on by any religion. It can find social comfort in religion, but it is always a personal choice of the individual. It is a choice to accept the will of the Father regardless of any laws imposed upon him by a religious social structure. At the moment of crossing to the other side it is only the individual and his Maker.

Marital Life – The Real World

When Jackie and I decided to marry we knew it would be rough and had even considered leaving town to avoid the problem. South America as missionaries was considered but South St. Louis was more to my liking. The Lord never prompted me to become soup for some tribes that did not know Him...there were others who had that gift. God bless them all, I know they will be rewarded. We all have different gifts from the Lord – being a missionary was not one of mine.

To our knowledge no priest who married had ever stayed in town and faced the music as it were. There may have been some, but we were unaware of this fact at the time. In fact, nothing was ever brought out publicly about any priest who married, either by the church or by the media. Well, Jackie and I decided to stay in St. Louis and keep our heads high.

There was nothing wrong with what we would do in God's eyes

and even four centuries before it was acceptable to the Church. It only became a church law in the Council of Trent around 1645 A.D. So it was settled. We would stay in town.

I contacted my classmate about my plan and we both decided that there is strength in numbers and he too would not run. Sooo...we married on the same day. The reaction by fellow clergy was mixed. Some wrote me saying get out of town and that I should be tarred and feathered. I was considered by some as a Judas Iscariot. Others blessed us, and in the year or so that followed also left the priesthood, married, and stayed in town. These thanked us for doing what we had done and said it did make it easier for them. I am sure that all of us suffered in one way or another. It was not easy for anyone who really desired the priesthood to be considered a failure. To my way of thinking, marrying in those days was the epitome of what a priest of God needed to do if so led. A true priest does not worry about what men may think, but of what God desires.

The reaction to my leaving and marrying was not really understood by non-Catholics who had the tradition of married ministers or clergy. As Shakespeare would say, "There was much ado about nothing." I was out to prove that a man could be a priest and still marry and make his way in the secular world as any other could do. I was doing it. I still think about what possessed me to give up walking ten feet off the ground and being worshiped by the Catholic population. I know what it was, and forty five years later with four wonderful children and a wonderful wife, I am glad I did it.

After the first months of marriage Jackie and I settled into the routine of adjustment to each other. We had purchased a home on three acres in the Fenton area when it was still unknown and country and began to build a home where there had been only a house. There were few possessions but they were adequate. There wasn't much money in those days and things have not changed over the years. We are sometimes amazed at how we made it, but agree it is the Lord's doing.

After a time the event of a married priest living in the area was not so miraculous and we weren't paid exceptional attention by anyone. At least that is what we thought. There were some who bore a grudge and acted upon it. But this un-Christian attitude was mainly from Catholics who didn't seem to know what Christianity was anyway. It was around the time of the Fourth of July after we had gone to bed that we heard a popping noise outside of our room air conditioner. I went outside to see what it could be and as I walked out the front door I noticed a car parked at the edge of the property. As I watched, it began to move forward down the road and would soon pass where I was standing on the front porch. As it moved I noticed that there were flickers of light in the car, which I soon found out, were matches. Perplexed as I was, it soon became evident what was going on. As the car became even with where I was standing two bottle rockets shot out at me and I heard the war cry... "That's for you, you son of a b!?!?!"

I didn't take the bottle rockets being shot near the house as personal, but the war cry seemed a little more directive. I was puzzled, to say only one of the emotions I felt. I did make up my mind to come out of the house to investigate anything in the future with more armament in case these folks had access to a howitzer. I found out later why there could be any antagonism toward me.

It seems as if the local pastor of the Catholic Church had somewhat disparagingly said something of my not being a human being and I was to be shunned by all good God-fearing Christians, especially Roman Catholics. When I found this out it explained why the Catholic neighbors would turn their heads when passing the house even though I would wave. I found this out after a year or so of living in the neighborhood. So much for the peaceful existence of homesteading in this rural area! This same pastor had sent word that I should not bring my newborn son to his church to be baptized. Somehow he must have forgotten that I was still an ordained priest and I really didn't need him for anything.

At the time I was not aware of what antagonisms may have been present in the church community, but I did know something was going on and chose to ignore it outwardly. Inside I was hurt and angry. For the first year, Jackie and I were isolated by the Roman Church. We had each other and knew that it would not be easy, but looking back on it; it was rougher for Jackie than for me. I had some anger to sustain me.

I must admit that over time things changed. The pastor apologized for his actions and admitted to my face that he could not have done what I did. He was of a different generation. His apology went so far as to personally greet me as he walked down the aisle as he came in to say Mass. (I still went daily for quite a while.) Time heals all wounds and it also healed us. Maybe the memories are there, but the anger and animosity is gone. I can blame no one for what they felt in those days. My neighbors became good friends after a time, and today Jackie and I are the old folks on the property with the barn with a lien on it. After all – it is over fifty years old.

We had decided early on that I would work and Jackie would stay at home and tend to the children and the house. It wasn't long after we were married that our first Joy arrived. Richard. How he survived doting and ignorant parents is a testimony to the love of God for each of us. No parent knows what to do with children. It happens a little when we become grandparents and then it is too late. Nobody listens anyway most of the time.

I was working as a salesman for a GE lighting distributor and tending to the outside of the house. We had almost three acres, and my farming ancestry must have kicked in because we soon had a young steer, chickens, ducks, and rabbits. Needless to say, I was very busy but loved it all and still do. Jackie was occupied with Richard, and son John was soon added to the mix. Another Joy to our life. Now with two sons, a sales job, and a small farm to attend to, I added a few goats to the menagerie. It was all right with Jackie because we always seem to be on the same page. Life was definitely busy and it was not always peaches and cream.

Like any marriage, we had (and still do) our disagreements and arguments, but it was all pretty normal. Since we were banished from the Catholic Church, and were not really accepted by the "good Catholics" we didn't attend church anywhere. By this time I wouldn't have gone to church anyway due to the fact that even if I agreed with the Church at that time, they wouldn't agree with me. A Mexican standoff. Jackie and I knew God and knew He wasn't working overtime in the Catholic Church, but we were too busy to really care.

Another Joy appeared in the form of Kathryn. The first girl and what a wonderful event that was. We now had two boys and a girl. We were both delighted and very blessed. At this time Jackie began to feel that we needed the Lord back in our life, and she began to get involved in the Charismatic movement of the Catholic Church. I was still not interested and would baby-sit while she attended church on Saturday nights. This got a little old very quickly. There had to be a better way of spending Saturday nights besides babysitting. There definitely was when our fourth Joy showed up named Aaron. I then began to think seriously about joining Jackie at Saturday night church. Charismatic or not, I would give the Charismatics a chance.

When Jackie and I got married we decided to have a lot of children. Maybe even seven or eight would be nice. We still had this idea after Richard. Then when John came along it went down to six. When Kate came along it went down to five. When Aaron came along it went down to who knows. They were all wanted and there were no mistakes, but there was one miscarriage that changed our attitudes. We call her Maureen because she and we needed a name for her no matter how long she was present with us. When we had the miscarriage with Maureen something happened that was what I would call a spiritual occurrence. We were both very concerned about a D and C, which Jackie had to undergo. She was scared and so was I as we sat and held hands in the hospital room waiting for the operating room to open. I promised her that I would be with her no matter what or where she would go, hoping to be able to comfort her and alleviate her fears and mine. The time came when she got on the gurney and was wheeled away down the hall and up the elevator to another floor. I felt totally horrible. I had been with her for the last three of our four children during the labor and birth, and I felt that this was equally if not more important than those times. I knew there was nothing I could do physically. But mentally was another option. I had heard about mental or spiritual or soul projection (you can call it what you will) and I would give it a try.

I got into a relaxed position in the chair I was in and began to still my mind. I kept trying to force my mind and thoughts to where Jackie was by being as quiet as my mind would allow me. Basically, as I recall, I was trying to be where she was. Suddenly I had an image of a clock, the kind that you see protruding from a wall so it can be seen from both sides of the hall. The time on the clock was 2:25 p.m. I went into the hall outside the room and looked up and down the hall. There was no clock anywhere, even in an adjoining intersecting hall.

I was a little puzzled and put it down as imagination. After all, it was only a fleeting glimpse. I seemed to relax more as I awaited Jackie's return, which was a few minutes later. She was all right and I was relieved. As I inquired about her experience, she said as she waited outside the operating room she suddenly became very relaxed and felt my presence. I asked her if there was a clock around her and she said there was one directly over her head. I asked if she had noticed a time when she felt relaxed. She said yes; it was 2:25 p.m. Coincidence? I think not.

Again Jackie and I got into the routine of having four children. Did I say routine? No way, Jose! There is no such thing as a routine with raising any child, but with four under twelve years old it is a circus of mental stress! But again, with the help of God we made it!

Jackie and I began to use our talents in helping out a former nun who ran what she called a Healing Clinic that basically was an Inner Healing Seminar which ran for nine weeks. It consisted of talks, group discussion, and prayer. We both found a great deal of satisfaction in this.

I was using my talents as a speaker and pastoral counselor, and Jackie was using her talent in prayer direction for women. I will be forever thankful to Sr. Cecilia Ann for giving me the opportunity to use my ministerlal talents at a time when I felt totally useless to the Lord, and not in keeping with my spiritual desires. It was due to her that I began to see that I could be of service to the Lord, and she used my talents and me where the Church did not because I got married. That's the Church's problem. They have lost a lot of tremendous talent due to their stubborn pride.

It was at this time that I began to get involved in the Charismatic Church against my will. I say "against my will" because basically I was what I would call a "head Christian." Anything that had to do with emotion was really not spiritual or Godlike. After all, Jesus was not emotional and a good priest would not allow himself to be emotional. I'm not sure where I picked that up, but after twelve years of seminary training for the priesthood, I think it might have had something to do with it. Jackie was very patient with my reluctance in attending a Charismatic Mass.

She did not push me at all, but there was something in me that desired and pulled me to it. I remember the first time I attended a Charismatic Mass.

The pastor of the church greeted me very warmly even though I was still considered persona non grata and was not supposed to be going to church anyway. He also did not believe the laws of the Church and has since left the Roman Church. But it was the first time in years that a brother priest who was still visibly active accepted me. I will never forget that warm greeting. I was feeling pretty comfortable as the Mass began. The music was beautiful and everyone was singing in tongues. It sounded like a choir of angels. Then it happened. At a particularly quiet part of the Mass, the man directly in front of me got hit with the Spirit.

He jumped up, raised his arms, and began to pray in tongues. That was it for me! I almost ran out of the church and headed for the side door. I did not breathe until I got outside. These people were crazy!! Jackie came outside and calmed my fears and I did go back in with much trepidation. That was over thirty years ago, and I must say I have really changed.

I now find it difficult to attend any service where there is not much arm raising or speaking in tongues or what I used to call hooting and hollering. Quiet time is for personal prayer and meditation.

My career as a supply salesman continued during this time. I went from retail sales to commercial and contractor selling which I liked a lot more. It left more time for me to be off work during the Christmas holidays and I could spend more time with the family. This was always the main focus of my life. To have a family always seemed to be most important to me because the family is the basis for society, and a good family would have to lead, almost as a necessity, to a good society. My attitude toward being a salesman was to always be on call for my customers. I was always only a phone call away and did not play the salesman game of going into the office late, crowing about how busy I was, going to lunch, making one personal sales call, and going back to the office and staying late in order to impress the boss (who probably played the same game when he was a salesman.)

I worked first thing in the morning and maximized my time even though it did not look like it. I worked from home and did not have to waste time. At the same time, when I could not be productive in selling I could be with the family and work in the garden and around the house. This meant that at times I would be working on the job until much later than those who only maintained office hours. I found it quite satisfying.

I never made much money, but the time with the family came first. The boss had already told me that I could be the manager of this major supply house – but then he picked another man to be sales manager and told me I could always go elsewhere. Being hardheaded and having what I wanted, which was not what everyone thought I should want, I stayed with the company in spite of the boss.

I really felt good about it when he gave me a list of small accounts to call on that should have insulted me and prompted me to leave. He didn't know me very well. The accounts were historically doing so little after a year with the company that they should have been erased from the books. Contrary to popular sales belief, since they were not capable of big sales, they should not require a sales person. I called on them anyway. You never know what can happen. Well, it did. One of the smallest accounts just happened to be a government supplier who was looking for an energy-saving light bulb. These were the beginning days of energy awareness. He told me of his need and that no one from our company had ever called upon him so he was going elsewhere. I made one of the largest sales of a new energy saving light bulb in the country. General Electric was so impressed that they made an ad in a national trade magazine about it with yours truly the featured salesman. I felt like I threw sand in the boss's face. Or was it something else in his face. No matter. I did something that not very many salesmen can do or did and I enjoyed the challenge and the results. No raise, but a lot of pride in doing the exceptional! Of course, I had been offered a job with General Electric directly but refused because of not wanting to travel or to be transferred. I made another presentation for Allen Bradley Control, which brought me another job offer, but turned that down also.

My first consideration was for the family and I don't regret it. Again, it would have meant more money but less concentration on the family presence.

All in all things were pretty good. The kids were all in school; we were all pretty healthy; and money was still tight. But within, there was still something that was gnawing on me and I wasn't sure what it was. I still did not feel fulfilled. I really was good at what I was doing, but something was not right. Then it hit me; I did not want to be a salesman the rest of my life. There would not be the security that I wanted, even though the security would be in me, and only in me. I had always enjoyed counseling people even before I was ordained, but when the opportunity was offered to me by the Archdiocese after ordination to go back to school for a counseling degree, I declined. I had enough of school and wanted to activate my priesthood, even though it did not last long. I don't do things the easy way, obviously, because now I wanted to go for a counseling degree and I would have to pay for it myself. Dumb all the way through! That is how I felt.

I first went to University of Missouri at the St. Louis campus to see about enrolling in their counseling program. The person in charge of the program told me that I was in all likelihood incapable of doing the program and he would not recommend me unless I could prove that I was capable. A real Catch 22. But then again, it was obvious that he did not want me in the program but if I could get a letter of recommendation from a doctor, a judge and a police official he might considerate it. It made no difference that I had already spent for years in graduate school. Looking back it seems as if he didn't care much for a so called ex-priest. I was crest fallen and in despair. I was forty seven years old and had more experience counseling than he had, and I couldn't get a degree in it. So much for UM. I really am glad that it didn't work with them. The Lord knew what should be after all, even though I cried much of the way home. Jackie was very supportive and suggested I try Webster University. I didn't have much hope but thought I may as well give it a try. The department head at Webster told me that I didn't need counseling experience, (here we go again, I thought) but I needed credentials and I was accepted with open arms into the counseling psychology department. More expensive than UM, but closer to home and a program better than they had at UM.

I signed up right away and then got really scared. I was older than most and I had the sales job and was doing counseling on the side, and now I was going to start a two-year program in addition to four children still at home.

Was I crazy? Yes. Sometimes it helps to be a little crazy. It took all of our meager savings to get through the program, and at times I knew I was crazy because I couldn't remember where I should go on Monday evenings – school, a sales meeting, or a counseling session. I would leave the house not sure of where I would wind up, but always remembered before I would get too far from home. Thank God. The first night of school I was a basket case. The students taking the course were at least twenty five years younger than me and I was really intimidated. Then the Lord came through. As I parked and got out of the car I saw a gentleman I knew who had also left the priesthood after I did and who thanked me for my leaving because it prompted him to leave and marry. He was on the staff at Webster and was taking the same orientation class that I was to take. We walked into the class together and I felt as if my father was with me on my first day of school. He was older than me too. I aced the two years scholastically and graduated in 1988. This was at the same time that the supply company gave me my outplacement package and I got fired. I walked right from the supply house office to my new counseling office and began the career that I knew was meant for me. I spent the next twenty three years doing what I really desired.

The 1990's were even tougher years monetarily, but at last I felt that I was doing what I was meant to do and it was very satisfying for me. Jackie was still very supportive and put up with much and doing with little. The kids were getting older, and we had used all the small savings we had acquired to get me through graduate school, so she went back to teaching. It was quite a help to us both.

I had thought that I would get a clientele of neurotic dissatisfied housewives and counseling would be a breeze. Wrong again!

Most of the clientele I had the first years were of feminine abuse which took a lot of time and effort. Nevertheless, I liked it because I felt the Lord was in charge and I was making a difference in lives and I had not felt that when I was wearing the Collar of a Priest. I always said that God was Edgar Bergen (a ventriloquist) and I was his dummy, Charlie McCarthy. How often that has been the case is innumerable. An emotional healing suggestion I offer for everyone has been that they are Spirits having a Human Experience and not the other way around. This is as true today as it was when I was counseling full time. My office was in Kirkwood and only a few minutes from the house. It was very convenient but the income was sparse. Since Jackie was also teaching it was almost adequate, but not quite. During this time I incorporated twice and both times the corporations failed for lack of finances. I think perhaps that the Lord was not in control, but I was and it wasn't what He wanted. That is hindsight, which I am very good at but not very good at foresight. (Hopefully, the Lord is working on that.) He did pull me out anyway.

Since our son, John, is VP of Boys and Girls Town of Missouri, he asked if I would like to work for them to supplement my income. I accepted the job as an outreach therapist and it was very interesting. It was also very frustrating and I left after four years. The child could be healed emotionally while on the campus but when they got home it was the same dysfunctional family situation that brought them to BGTM. While with them I set up a program as a crisis counselor at the Bourbon High School, a function that I continue to this day.

Shortly after graduating in 1988 I by chance, found out that I could be licensed as a social worker in the State of Missouri by being grandfathered in under new rules. I took advantage of this and am still licensed as a Licensed Clinical Social Worker. This has allowed me to take most medical insurances from my clients. It's also a practice that I discontinued due to the lack of office help and the problems with the insurance procedures in getting paid.

I left BGTM around 2002 and continued in a private practice until around 2005 when I retired and began to only work by appointment, a practice I continue today. This is a somewhat brief synopsis of my career to this point.

Richard A. Money

The Kingdom of God

How many times are we told the kingdom of God is within? Over and over, and – where is within? How do we go within? Meditation? Yes. That's one way. But why do we say the KINGDOM of God? What is a kingdom? Where are the kings? Do we understand what a kingdom really is? A kingdom is an archaic word depicting kings, queens, knights, etc. What does it mean today to modern youth and to our modern culture? Nothing. It is a word from the past, a word from the Bible that really does not mean a whole lot to any of us. It symbolizes King Arthur and Queen Guinevere. Camelot. Not much else. What did it mean in the days of the Christ? Jesus used it because it was understandable to the culture of his day. It meant the Roman Empire, the kingdoms of the Jewish and Arabian peoples. Kingdoms were of kings and queens, understandable to the people of his day.

What was Jesus trying to tell us all? It was not only for the Jews and peoples of His time, but for all mankind.

GOD IS THE FATHER OF US ALL. WE ARE ALL HIS CHILDREN AND AS SUCH WE ARE TO LOVE ONE ANOTHER AS BROTHER AND SISTER. WE

ARE TO BE AS ONE FAMILY, A FAMILY UNITED UNDER ONE FATHER, REGARDLESS OF RACE, COLOR OR CREED.

God wants nothing more than to be a Father, as a natural father wants to care for His children, to give them what they need, but to also give them the abundance of a Father's heart. He wants to give them more than what they could need for; to see them flourish and prosper; to see them grow and pass on to others what He has given them; to love their brothers and sisters as He has loved them all; to be united in a familial situation to a exclusion of no one. Basically, the message of Jesus was that the Fatherhood of God was to be the same as an earthly father would want for his children.

As all children count on the love of the father, no matter what the circumstances they would find themselves in, they count on their father to care, give, and provide for them whatever the need. They want a father who would not condemn, not command, but who would support and guide in times of need and stress. They want a father who would be present wherever and whenever he was needed, and yet allow for freedom to express feelings and hopes for individual growth. The KINGDOM WITHIN is just the relationship that God the Father has with each of us that expresses the relationship of the Father with each of us both corporately and individually. It is that we are united with the Father as one family under his direction and care and love. It is the understanding and awareness that we are all one under the Father, and as children we are united with brothers and sisters of all fellow humans under one Father in LOVE.

The Evolution of Religion

As the reader may have guessed by now, this is not a scholarly work filled with references and notes. It is a book about my opinions and promptings that I believe we all have that come from the Holy Spirit. Hopefully, I have paid attention to His promptings.

Recently, there have been two major occurrences in the 21st century which seem to have prevented us from having a defined line of knowledge from the ancient writings and teachings of centuries past. We are just becoming aware of our world and cultures from the past. There have been thousands of manuscripts and writings from the ancient past that have lain dormant for centuries. As they have been discovered they have thrown light on what we are experiencing in our world today.

The two historical occurrences are the burning of the library of Alexandria and the 4th century burning of the books of the Bible by Constantine. In the Alexandrian event, all known manuscripts in the world at that time were destroyed. These numbered in the thousands. In the 4th century, there were thousands of books and manuscripts written about Jesus and His times that were destroyed. Constantine decided that there was too much confusion and he codified the Bible to the books we have today. Some of these manuscripts and writings are in the Vatican Library locked away and forbidden to be seen. What are they and why are they not made public? I certainly don't know.

In 1946, on the shores of the Dead Sea, there was a major discovery of manuscripts and writings that date back to the days and times of Jesus, and even before His life. There are over 25,000 pieces of writings and full manuscripts that shed a great deal of knowledge. Not all of them to this day have been totally studied.

What we have learned from these writings is that there have been other gospels written about Jesus by the Apostles. The gospel of Thomas is one such gospel. In this gospel, there is a focus as Jesus being the Light that has come into the world. My point is that there is much we do not know about the life of Jesus that seems to have been lost and suppressed and may now just be coming to light 1,700 years later. What I will be offering as a proposition or as a possibility is heresy. But there are cultural and historical facts to prove what I am saying could be true, not to mention the facts of space and time.

Let us take, for example, the story of the birth of Jesus. We all know it. He was born in a stable of a virgin. Angels sang HOSANNA, and wise men came from India, China and points east following a star that led them to a king, so they brought kingly gifts. From some of the knowledge today of the past literature discovered at the Dead Sea, this story is a Hebrew MIDRASHIM. What this is, in so many words, is a story or fable that tells a truth in what I would call a poetic way (for lack of better words). The meanings of the story are true but the details leave a lot to be desired. For example, it only took three days for the kings to get to Jesus. Wow, they must have had some really fast camels! They came from east of Nazareth by camel, supposedly from the kingdoms of India, China, and who knows where in three days. Faster than American Airlines today. Just kidding. But really, why was Jesus' birth in a stable in this story – to tell the truth that he was born of a man and woman of lowly birth, and that he really was a king and was to be honored by kings. The gifts themselves were gifts of royalty. There is much more that could be said of these types of stories or fables that are in the Bible, and believe me, I have not studied them all, nor do I have the capability to do so. As I have said, I am not a scholar, but I do believe in common sense and the revelations of God in Jesus' life to me seem to be more plausible than that which I have been raised with in everyday Christianity.

What I am going to say now is only going to be a WHAT IF... I am not espousing a fact or a new way of thinking. Least of all, I do not want to start a new religion. So the Pope can relax now, as can all the major religions of the world. There are more than enough of them!

WHAT IF...Jesus was born in the normal way as all men are born? Why did it have to be of a virgin? Why did it have to be miraculous? Was the story of this birth to prove that He was God and someone special?

WHAT IF...Jesus had a normal childhood, but in his early years, He began to become aware of something within Him that prompted Him to believe that there was a Power within Him that others did not have or know about? As He grew in wisdom and grace as the Bible says, could it have been an Inner Awareness given by the Holy Spirit for His growth in those 30 years that we supposedly know little about?

WHAT IF...He was seen to be so normal that no one recognized Him as someone special until He began to teach about the Father from where He came, and the Father from whom we are all descended?

WHAT IF...He came not to die, but to live a life that manifested the life of the Father, a life that was filled with love and the knowledge that, because we all have the same Father of love and mercy, we are all brothers. This was the basic teaching of Jesus?

WHAT IF...there are so many more truths about this man that were written by the Apostles, that we see him as a man as we all are, but given a great inner awareness by the Father to reveal the Father to the world? Would this destroy our belief that Jesus was the Son of God? More importantly, could it not give us the knowledge that He wanted to impart to the world, that we are all sons of God and that we can do even greater things than He did if we follow His way?

WHAT IF...we stopped looking at Jesus as the ONLY SON OF GOD and realized that WE TOO ARE SONS AND DAUGHTERS OF GOD. Isn't this what He really wanted of us all, to realize the Divinity that lives in all of us? As our first catechism says, we are made in the Image and Likeness of God. Simple isn't it? Are we aware of it? And what do we do about it? I know, let's make a religion out of it and make some laws that force us to act that way.

Seriously though, haven't we been childlike in our conception of God the Father, and to a certain extent, haven't we been childlike in our belief of Jesus the Christ? Perhaps, in the years to come, we may realize the total picture of our relationship to God and to the One who revealed the Father to us. In the beginning we as humans had a fear of God. He was in lightning, thunder, fire and powerful storms. It was fear for thousands of years that motivated our relationship with God. Fear and sacrifice ruled how we worshipped God. This continued until the time of Jesus, who came not to bring fear, but to bring the knowledge that God is really a God of Love and Mercy and Forgiveness. But the point is, did Jesus know in the very beginning of His existence in this world, that this was His job and that He was to reveal the Father to the rest of the world? Or perhaps, was it a growth of the Holy Spirit within Him that revealed the knowledge of the Father? Did He struggle as we do with becoming aware of ourselves? Did He have the same doubts as we do as HE GREW in wisdom and in grace? Was he fully HUMAN? Yes, and that answers the question. We have made His awareness of Divinity within Himself from the beginning of His birth. Was He aware that He dirtied His diaper and called for His virgin mother to change it for Him? We have made Jesus of Nazareth a God, and in a sense, lost contact with who we all are.

By that I mean, in trying to prove the Divinity of Jesus, we have made Him a person who is so disconnected from us as human beings, that we may feel lost. The early fathers of Christianity with their attempts to prove that Jesus was the Son of God, I believe, did this. It was a good try, as it were, but I believe it may have done more harm today than good. Jesus was a full human being, totally and entirely. He suffered the same things we all do; doubt, fear, anger, etc., all the emotions that humans feel in this life. Jesus is not OUT THERE apart from us because He is God. God is not OUT THERE apart from us – He lives within us, which is the main idea that Jesus came to reveal to humanity.

I feel that in the overemphasizing by the early Church, the Divinity of Jesus, (and this may not have been an overemphasizing at all, but a necessity for the times) that today we need to see and feel the presence and message of Jesus. That message is that we are not alone and lost, and that God is not somewhere OUT THERE, but is a real presence within us. Would we not act differently if we felt and knew that there is a Presence within us that can guide us, care for others and us, and that it is a gift we have for all eternity? That same Holy Spirit which guided Jesus is with us today. I believe most of us don't know it even though He told us that when He left that Spirit would come and remain with us.

To say that we are God scares most people, but does not a son or daughter share the genes, the life and most of what the father has? Is it not fair to say that being in the image and likeness of God, we share in whatever God is? The Son is not the Father, nor is the Father the Son, but in reality can we not say they are the same? How simple it seems to me, but how simple I am. The wave is not the ocean and the ocean is not the wave. Try and separate them.

I believe that if we can be quiet enough in meditation, the Father will send us more knowledge of Jesus and how we can relate to Him. I also think that we have spent too much time in following religious practices and we have lost sight of the personal relationship that leads to salvation and peace of the soul. That personal relationship is not all – at times religion is also necessary, but it seems that today there needs to be a balance of the two which is not evident to the majority of people, especially in the Western culture. We are surrounded by noise, and we sometimes act as if the rituals we perform are the saving elements in religion. They are not. The rituals without the personal awareness and desire of the individual are nothing but rituals that mean nothing to the person. This is not an attempt to deny the social benefits of common sharing of Christianity. After all, did not Jesus say where two or more are gathered in My name I will be there? Or did He really say that? Maybe it was a translator of the Bible.

I am being facetious now, and do not mean to be so ornery. What I mean is that the Bible is not wrong, but it is not complete. There are many things that do not fit in it, example being that Jesus had to say many things that are not in the Bible as we know it. There could be and probably are many things that are left out, and I believe that if we knew more about some of the things that He may have said, we would feel closer to Him as a human and not so separated from the Father.

To a certain extent I believe that we are on the cusp, as it were, of a new generation of religion and belief in Jesus and the Father. There seems to be a feeling of something coming that will reveal spirituality more than the past two thousand years. People are becoming more spiritually aware. This is not to say that everyone is coming to this spiritual awareness, but a greater number are becoming more spiritual and aware. The earth is changing and so are the people living on it, because we are all one. The year 2012 is not the end of it all, but the beginning of a New Age. I believe that this new age is already here and we don't know it yet.

I have entitled this section the *Evolution of Religion* because I believe that today, and in the days to come, we will have a total picture of the last two thousand years and of the age to come. This will put religion in perspective and the Age of Spirituality will flourish. We have evolved from a people of fear of God and childish rituals to a people who know who they are as children of God, and are aware of the Power within them. I believe it to be an era of peace and love but not a Utopia, for although we are children of God, we still can make choices that can separate us from Him. The choice is up to us. God does not force by law, but by love and freedom.

Kansas City and Healing

Seminar

In 2003 I attended a healing seminar in Kansas City that was paid for by a friend, Michael Butler. He and his wife, Tina, also attended the seminar. It was not a religious event at all. It was far from religion. In fact there was an injunction to not say anything religious during the various workshops which were held as part of the event. It was called RECONNECTIVE HEALING SEMINAR and was given by a man called Eric Pearl, who was basically a chiropractic doctor by trade. His reason for the seminar was that he was told by angelic voices to start this type of work with others. Sounded wacko to me, but what do I know, and besides, Mike was paying for it plus the lodging. I read his book, and I believe Mr. Pearl was acting in good faith. After all, this is a new age and he was talking about energy work which, in quantum physics, is what the world and this universe is all about.

In the two-day seminar we were told to heal people by moving our hands over the body of the person in a circular or sweeping motion from the head or from the feet to the opposite part of the body, never touching the body or saying anything at all. We were not even to ask what part of the body needed to be healed, but allowing the energy to be felt by the hands of the practitioner when he was in the area which needed to be healed. At first, I thought that this guy was going to try and sell us ocean front property in Arizona. But again, I was wrong. He was for real! In his demonstrations before we were involved in the workshops, time and again he caused arms to move that could not move, backs to become limber, etc. I began to wonder if there were not plants in the crowd for his demonstration. It was not possible for this kind of healing to take place with people. At least, this was my opinion. In the workshops, we all worked with one another, and during this time whenever I was working with someone, they felt very peaceful and relaxed. No big deal. But there were some who felt the energy flowing through them from the hands of the one waving his or her hands over them.

This was getting more interesting all the time. After two days of this I was becoming a believer. After all, I had heard of healings taking place by the therapist connecting with the patient's disease or problem by use of the energy of the surrounding atmosphere or by the therapist's connection with the energy itself. I still don't know how to explain it, but it seemed to work from the reports I had heard about. I was becoming a believer and could hardly wait to try it out, but I didn't know on whom or when it could be used. I was soon to find out.

In another part of this writing, I recounted the event with my daughter-in-law who had undergone a horrible delivery experience with her firstborn son. The healing seminar was held in Kansas City, as I said, and my son Aaron and his wife Carolyn live in the suburb of Blue Springs. On the way home I stopped by to say hello and was told of the pain she was going through and the problem. I asked her if I could try something that was demonstrated at the seminar and she consented.

I did what I had seen done at the seminar, waving my hands over her body and getting in touch with the energy of the body as I had been told. When I did this at the seminar, relaxation took place with the object of the demonstration, the pretend patient, becoming very relaxed. This happened to Carolyn as well. After the session I asked how she was feeling and she commented that she felt very relaxed. I am a clinical hypnotherapist and I thought that this procedure would be less work than verbally putting someone under hypnosis. I thought that this might have possibilities after all. The only difference in this session with my daughter-in-law was that during this session I prayed quietly, invoking the healing power of God through Jesus and with the union of the Holy Spirit, but not saying anything out loud. This was contrary to what Mr. Pearl advised, but I believed, and still do, that all healing is of God. He may use energy to heal, but He is still in charge. Carolyn felt very relaxed after the session and we thought it was not wasted time. Two days later Aaron called to tell me that Carolyn had no pain at all and felt completely fine.

To tell the truth, I was amazed. It seemed like this stuff really could work, but God and Jesus and the Holy Spirit have to be added to the mix. Since that time I have prayed with people and healings have taken place along with relaxation during the session. It seems to me that it is necessary to get in touch with God, who actually does the healing, while using the energy. This has worked for everyone I have prayed with, but I do not speak out loud or say anything. Only I know what I am praying. I don't feel that the healer has to scream out loud and invoke God verbally. This may be necessary in some cases and I am not an expert, but what I have done has worked for me every time. I hope it continues.

The Love of God Named

Jesus

We know from all that Jesus has revealed to us about the Father that we are loved by Him. We also know that the Father sent Jesus to this planet to reveal the Father to us, and also that the Father wanted Jesus to reveal just how much the Father loved Jesus and us. So much so that Jesus became man and did all that men do, so that we could see it very clearly.

Yet for nineteen centuries we have concentrated on the fact that the Father sent Jesus to die for us. How could a loving God, who we know is a loving Father, send his ONLY BEGOTTEN SON to a place to die so that we may be saved? Doesn't this relate to the Old Testament viewpoint that sacrifice is how God is appeased?

Doesn't this hearken to the Mayan manner of worshipping the Sun (which is light) and beheading people? Human sacrifice. Have we not said for so long that God the Father does not demand human sacrifice, and yet, we talk about the BLOOD OF THE LAMB WHICH HAD TO BE SACRIFICED OR SPILLED THAT WE MIGHT BE SAVED? Where is the consistency? Where has Christianity departed from the Old Testament language? Have we really looked at Jesus the MAN-GOD in the sense of what He really came to do? Was he primarily a God who came to die? That seems to have been the focal point of Christianity that I have grown up with all my life.

Yes, Jesus did die. A very cruel death to be sure. But weren't hundreds or maybe even thousands killed the same way He was? Were there not two other humans crucified with him on the same day as his crucifixion? His death in itself was not unique. What then was unique about Jesus? It was His entire life on the earth. It was His message about the Love of the Father and the subsequent brotherhood of all men because of the Father's Love held in common.

Should we not be focused more on His teachings on this earth during His time here rather than His death on the cross? This type of death was common to a lot of men. What was uncommon about Jesus was His message and WHO HE WAS. To me it is a shame that our focus has been on the negative instead of the positive. Historically, I can see why it was a normal transition for the apostles and the fathers of the early Church to consider Jesus in the light of the Old Testament. But in today's world, at least in my mind, we are missing the point of His Life.

We could apply this same attitude to a great many things that we attribute to Jesus' life, and be missing the point. Didn't the early Church (not the apostolic times but the times of the Church Fathers) degrade women? It wasn't until the 19th century that women could even vote. And of course, in Jesus' day, every woman He seemed to know was a prostitute or was one beneath the station of men. The culture of the day was such, and the monks that translated the early writing probably added their own views of women.

This last is my opinion and I am not an expert, but culture and human nature would seem to verify it. Let the scholars decide. After all I am only a mere salami, but one who has, perhaps, some special spice.

Religion and Evolution

A few weeks ago I read a story about Columbus and the Discovery of America. It is commonly believed that Columbus set sail to prove that the earth is round, and that he set out with three ships to prove it. My feeling was that there were four ships, but one fell off the edge. Let's start this off with a laugh...we are going to need it.

In the article, I read that everyone in Columbus's day knew that the earth was round. Aristotle had come to that conclusion about two thousand years earlier because he noted the shape of the shadow the earth left on the moon was round. As the story goes, Columbus did meet with some scholars, but it was not about the flatness of the earth but about the size of the earth. He thought it was smaller than it really is.

The story about Columbus setting off to discover a round earth was written by Washington Irving who wrote LEGEND OF SLEEPY HOLLOW, RIP VAN WINKLE, and other short stories. In 1828 he wrote the story of Columbus and how he set out to prove the earth was round because a group of scholars said it was flat. It was a fictional short story in a history book that he wrote about Columbus, but the majority of the people liked it and the book became a best seller. Irving's romanticized version of the heroics of Columbus made good reading and the people enjoyed it. They really wanted to believe it so it became a tale that was historically correct and handed down to the present day. It seems that only a few more enlightened people know the truth. I was not one of them, but that is no surprise.

Anyway, this got me thinking. What if the same thing could be said about a great many incidents of the Bible as religious scholars handed it down to us? Everyone who writes colors their stories and writings with their own perspectives and cultural inclinations. (All except me, who is very exacting and concise in all I say or write. Believe that, and I do have some ocean front property in Arizona that you can have real cheap!) It is almost common knowledge since the discovery of the Dead Sea Scrolls that there are many ancient writings that have gone unnoticed until recently, and that a great many of them are in secret places guarded by the religious leaders of our day. I say common knowledge and that may not be true. Most people do not care, but might if it were talked about more. Jesus Himself could, perhaps, have written some of these writings. Some scholars give this view some credibility but it doesn't make any difference. They seem to be authentic viewpoints of the days in which Jesus lived. As we have noted by discovering the Christmas story to be a Midrashim, could there not be many more stories which teach an eternal truth but which, in fact, are poetic or mythical in detail? Could it be that for two thousand years we have focused on the details of the stories in the Bible and have forgotten what its meaning really is and what it was meant to do? Again, I am not trying to grind an axe or debunk anything or anyone, but I really am questioning as I believe many are doing today. This is true especially of the educated youth of the day. There does seem to be a movement afoot of trying to discover the truth no matter what it is. In the writings long ago of men like Pere Teilhard de Chardin, there is an

142

evolution of thought where science and religion meet. It is called the OMEGA POINT. But it will take an open mind to reach it and we, at least in the present, have not.

Let's assume for a moment that Jesus of Nazareth was not called Jesus. Let's say his name was George of Jordan, or Michael of Michigan. Would it make any difference? Would it make any difference if he was named Urg of Urantia and came in a space ship? Would His message be any different or would He be saying the same thing? What does it matter, really, if He was married or single? Would He speak differently? Would the meaning and course of His life and what He came to reveal to us change? Why would it? Since He and all of us are spirits, would His spiritual message be different? Would He then say that none of us are of God, and that we are not all sons of God?

And what if we studied the teachings of the Buddha, of Mohammed and Krishna, and they all said the same thing that Jesus said but in a culturally different way? What if all of the above were really Avatars, not the ones in the James Cameron movie, but spirits sent by God to raise the level of Man's awareness about their Creator and how they need to act and grow as they walk this planet. What if they all said about the same thing in different ways, the only difference being that Jesus revealed what the Creator Father wanted from us in specific detail? Remember, before you take me to the guillotine, I am only positing possibilities and hypotheses. Could it be that we need to evolve in our viewpoint of God to a higher level than the almost superstitious religions that we have adhered to for centuries? I don't know, but I feel that we are headed for a higher level of Divine Awareness.

Let's assume again, that as Jesus is the Son of God He has revealed to us that we too are all sons of God. If we think about it we were told from early on that we were made in the image and likeness of God. What does that mean?

Are we only a part image, and what part? Are we a part likeness, and again what part? Are we as Jesus is, made of the Substance of God, the Mind of God, and the Hands of God in this world? Are we to carry on the teaching of Jesus and fulfill our destiny as mandated by the Creator Father, or do we believe that it is up to Jesus to do, while we sit passively by? I can believe that God created me and sent me into this world to do something for Him. Unfortunately, when I got here I forgot what it was and my journey here became a matter of an evolving awareness of what it is and how to do it by trial and error.

Could it not be that Jesus is really the Son of God, and that we are all sons of God because we have become brothers to Jesus as He has become a human like unto us? Is it heresy to say He is a Divine Spirit and that we too can be Divine Spirits? We have the capability of being Divine Spirits as we have the same capacity as Jesus has. Did He not say that "If you do as I do, you shall do what I do, and even greater things than I do"? Or is this just the gospel writer's wish that Jesus would have said it? I don't know.

What I do know is this: the message of Jesus and the reason for His existence in the world was to reveal our God as a loving Father for all mankind, and therefore we are all brothers and need to act in the same love for all men. It was not to create more laws. It was not to have a special religion, race or country. I believe that this in its simplicity was all the Father, through Jesus, meant to have happen.

Evolution of physical species is not the only evolution on this planet. There is also the evolution of thought. It is obvious if we stop and think, yes, think. We do not think the same way as we have in the past. Do we think we can go to the planet Mars or travel to the stars? Are we beginning to believe that we have the power within us to change the world by thought and prayer (no matter what you may call prayer)?

Was Jesus a Human Sacrifice?

What I am about to say is probably heresy in most religious circles. The thoughts that I have are just that – thoughts. I am not espousing a new way of thinking because I don't even have a real grip on the old way of thinking. I'm not sure if I can even think at all sometimes. Like the old saying goes, "Did you ever stop to think, and then forget to start?" I wonder. Well, here goes.

What really was Jesus all about? We call Him the Son of God, the Son of Man, the Savior of the world, the God who came to die for us and without Him there is no salvation. The God who became a man... the message seems to be that Jesus was a God-Man who had to come and die so that we would be saved. Saved from what? Of course, going to hell.

Which is what – separation from God? O.K. Now I get it. God has a Son who is a part of God, and now He sends this son to Earth to die because if this son dies we are saved? Does this sound a lot like the human sacrifices of the past? It does to me. But what if we look at the process of this major event in a different way.

The plan of our salvation does not rest upon whether or not Jesus died, but upon the message that He brought to the world. What was the message? The Creator Father, the Almighty, no matter what He is called in various cultures in this world, this Supreme Being who created us, created out of love. He still loves us and is a loving Father Creator who asks that we treat our fellow human beings as brothers under His one Fatherhood. It seems to me that's all. The problem, as I see it, is that we have complicated the message to the extent that we have really lost the message. We don't see the forest for the trees.

What if Jesus were an alien coming to this world to reveal who and what we are and are to be like in this universe?

Would it make any difference? Would the message be the same, or would it be different? Is it our perspective, that because Jesus would not be a religious figure, the message would not be true or a real revelation from some being from another planet or universe? The world we live in is not the real world. The real world is the spirit world. The "real us" is the soul, not the body. The Supreme Being is not a body but a spirit, and for lack of a better analogy, His Son is also a spirit. This Spirit we call Jesus. Jesus came to tell us, who also are spirits, that if we carry on the love of the Supreme Spirit we shall live forever in love with the Father. Jesus left us another Spirit when He went back home. We call it the Holy Spirit. He said this Spirit would help us love one another as brothers under one Father. This seems pretty simple to me, but I am probably a simpleton. Again, as Shakespeare said, "There is much ado about nothing." Or, we have complicated the activity of God with a lot of things that don't make any difference and only confuse the issue. The problem with all of this is that *we have a choice as to whether or not we believe the message of Jesus.*

The choice is not do we believe or do not believe in Jesus the God-Man Spirit, but whether or not we believe His message. His intent was not to come into this world to die. That was inherent in the fact that He became a man and all men die, or at least seem to, after original sin (my question). Our salvation does not depend upon His death in this world, which would be a natural occurrence, but upon the message that He brought. I feel that we have focused upon the death of Jesus and have somewhat forgotten the importance of the message. I may be off base, but this is the impression I have gotten over the years. If I have gotten that impression then, perhaps, others have too. But again, I must admit that I don't think like most people. At least that is what those who know me best would say.

It seems to me that we have focused on the fact that we must believe in Jesus as God Man or Son of God to be saved. We have spent centuries trying to prove that Jesus was the Son of God. Of course, this would add credibility to His message, but then, maybe we have forgotten the message and this would be contrary to what Jesus would desire.

Perhaps some of the miracles that Jesus was supposed to have performed were not really miracles at all but natural occurrences that seemed miraculous to his followers. If this were true, and I am not saying that it is true but is possible, then some may say, therefore, He was not really the Son Spirit of God at all. Then His message would not be true. Throw out the baby with the bath water!!!

Richard A. Money

Salvation does not depend upon whether or not Jesus is the Son of God, but upon the choice we make to follow His message. We cannot BE Jesus. His personality was unique as was His mission. But if we follow the message He gave us and look upon our brother humans as one under the one Father, we can then be sure that we are doing what Jesus asked of us. For all of us it is a matter of choice that may be founded upon belief in Jesus as God, but ultimately it is up to us in following His message as to how we spend eternity. PURE AND SIMPLE!

Healing the Human Doubt

Today is the day that I almost gave up writing about healing. I had a great deal of doubt about having the gift of physical healing. I know of several people who had cancer and were told it was gone, only to find out that it had returned. I know that God will do the healing and it is not the individual who prays for the healing that affects it, but I began to have doubts as to whether or not I would be able to be a part of this healing process.

Because of the help of a close friend, I began to realize that I was making myself the gauge of the healing process. My own ego or my sense of insecurity was foremost in my mind. The process and mystery of God was secondary to my wishes. My question to myself was, why pray for healing for someone if they are not going to be healed, and again, how can I presume to write about this healing process when I don't know enough about it? His reply to me was: Could I be strong enough and secure enough to be satisfied with a partial process? It just isn't black and white. My personality leans to black and white: Gray is non-existent a lot of the time in my thinking. If God has graced me with the healing gift at times, why must I determine that it must work all the time? God is still a mystery and I cannot forget that in many things, especially when praying for physical or any kind of healing. I can only do what I feel called or urged to do in my spirit. To have doubts is human nature but this is when faith needs to take over, faith in the promises and words of Jesus. It is faith not only on the part of the person being prayed with, but also on the part of the praying healer. It is faith to believe that no matter what the outcome of this prayer; it needs to be prayed. It is faith to be satisfied with a partial answer and not depend upon the outcome of the healing prayer. The dependence upon the outcome is an easy trap to fall into. It is black and white thinking. No matter what happens, the Lord is in control and it does not depend on the prayer no matter how good it is.

I have heard ministers say that God does not will that anyone get sick. I can agree with that, but why then do they get sick and sometimes die from the sickness? Is it semantics to say that He does not will it but does allow it? By allowing the sickness or affliction He has a better plan, even though I do not see it. Again, it is a matter of faith in the Mystery of God. How does a mortal solve the Mystery of God? We don't. We just live with it. We do the best we can and accept a partial healing or what seems to be none at all to our eyes, but believe that God knows best. (In my case, I am sure that Jesus has a sense of humor. After all, I act like I know what's best for everyone concerned!) In a sense, a healing prayer that doesn't seem to cause a healing to take place can be for the benefit of the one that is praying for the healing, that one being the one supposedly doing the healing on behalf of God.

It points to humility that we all must have, even when we may be present at the times that God miraculously Does His Thing.

There Are Dreams and

There Are Visions

I now believe that this was a vision, not just a dream. In the past four years I have had many dreams, but now I realize that some were visions and not just dreams. I am beginning to see the difference. The vision leaves with a feeling and a memory that doesn't fade and feels as if something is coming. For example, consider the following.

About three years ago while on vacation in Florida with my son and his family, I had a dream, or so I thought at the time. My massage therapist came to me and said that she was going to show me what was going to happen. We went to a place that I recognized as West County. The land was barren except for piles of cleared debris. Bulldozers and earthmovers were working.

Obviously, they were clearing the land for something to be built there. I asked her what it was, and she replied that it was to be a Disneyland. I was very disappointed because I expected it to be something real, and not a fairyland. I was so upset that I said I needed to talk to Joe, her husband who was a land developer. I went looking for him, and after going through various rooms in his company's building, I found his office. There were papers on his desk but he was not there and no one knew where he was. I awakened and felt a terrible sadness. What I wanted to see did not exist. My disillusionment was so great that I felt like crying and the feeling stayed with me all day long. My disappointment and depression were very deep. The prophecies I had received several times of being a healer and pastor were a sham – that is how I felt. This feeling lasted several days. About a week later I had another dream or vision.

It was: I was walking through a pasture among a herd of cattle and calves, painting the calves as I walked through. Jackie was with me but was not prominent in the dream.

Someone else was leading me and we were heading for a building in the woods. When we got near the building I saw that it was white with a large stained glass window. Seemed like a church. My guide led me in and then left, and I was surrounded by many young people. We were in what I recognized as a non-denominational church. There were offices downstairs and to the side. The stage was filled with sound equipment and microphones. The young people asked me if I was the new pastor. I replied that I didn't know. I asked where I was and was told that I was forty miles from Pacific, MO. In a second, I calculated that it was Cuba, MO. I then asked what was the name of this church and was told it was on a sign out front. I went out and the sign read: ANAHEIM LUTHERAN CHURCH. It made no sense to me. The young people went about their work making banners and the dream ended. Upon awakening I was really confused. I asked my son who had been to California, what was in Anaheim. He responded DISNEYLAND. At this point I was really confused.

I stayed that way for a couple of months. Jackie was working at Pacific High School at the time and I had been working in the Cuba area for many years calling on RCF homes.

What was going on? Several months passed and we attended Destiny Church in Des Peres. At one service the pastor mentioned that he had just returned from a church called CHANGE OF HEART in Cuba. We passed that church many times as we went down to our son's farm in St. James, MO. After the service Jackie suggested we stop by and see the church. I said no. I wanted to go squirrel hunting after we checked on the cattle that Saturday for my son. The next day I was working in the Cuba area, so I thought maybe I would check it out on my own.

As I drove down the lane for about half of a mile, I came to this little white church. Looking through the doors I could see sound equipment and microphones on the stage.

I thought that this might be more than a coincidence (which I do not believe in anyway), so I thought we should check it out on Saturday when we were to come down to St. James. Jackie agreed, but was somewhat confused as to why I had changed my mind.

We drove down the lane and it was then that I realized on both sides of the road were pastures. The cows were gone I subsequently found out, but it was definitely a pasture. We were coming closer to the church and I remarked to Jackie, if there were someone there who would lead us in, this would be more than a coincidence. SURE ENOUGH, THERE WAS A PERSON CLEANING THE GRAVEL OFF THE SIDEWALK. I stopped the car and went to talk to him. I found out that it was a non-denominational church and was aligned with LIFE CHRISTIAN CHURCH where we normally attended. He mentioned that he had thyroid cancer but it had been healed, but seemed to be coming back. Because I felt impelled to do so, I told him about my vision and what was said at Destiny Church. He became very excited and asked if I would like to meet the pastor who was inside.

This was freaky to me and, of course, I said yes. We went in and I recounted the dream I had and why we were here. At this point both the pastor and I were in tears and felt that something was going on that was bigger than both of us. Jackie and I agreed that we needed to come back to this church and we did. We are considered members of this church although at this time we go to both LIFE CHRISTIAN and CHANGE OF HEART. The man who led us in did have a recurrence of thyroid cancer, and he was prayed with by a group of people at Destiny church. His cancer was healed and to this day it has not recurred. COINCIDENCE?

I STILL BELIEVE SOMETHING IS GOING ON. I today have a counseling office in the church and the pastor and his wife have become good friends.

Prayer

I am not an expert on prayer. I really don't use any formula, even when praying for someone for a special intention or healing. To me it seems that God knows my heart even better than I do, and that is enough for Him. I believe that Gratitude is the best prayer that we have, because God is immutable and even though I know that some things happen because we pray for them, I'm not sure that it depends on my saying a prayer for it to be efficacious. What I mean is; the words themselves, said to myself, I feel will not change God's mind. But He is either immutable or He is not.

What I do believe is that my intentions or feelings are true prayer. Saying words without meaning in the heart or the emotions would seem to me to be useless. But I have to admit that I really don't know. Maybe I didn't study my theology enough.

I do believe that prayer is very necessary no matter what the situation or event. Prayer opens up the soul for a larger and deeper capacity for spiritual awareness whether the prayer is answered or not. This would seem to be the case whether the prayer is for a healing that does not seem to take place or for one that is physically evident. We benefit personally by praying no matter what the outcome. Who could not use a greater spiritual capacity?

Since true or real prayer comes from the heart, then it would follow that the prayer should come from one's own heart and soul. It does not have to be a formula written by someone else, but a conversation in one's own personal words, speaking as it were to a personal father who does care and is listening to what we have to say. Unfortunately, this is not always the case, because we do not trust ourselves or we do not trust that the Father or Jesus or the Holy Spirit would listen to us speaking in our own words.

If we look at the prayers of Jesus, those that are recorded are few. In fact, the only prayers of Jesus are found in the gospel of John. One is called Jesus' priestly prayer as He prays for those who the Father has given Him. This priestly prayer seems to be the only prayer recorded as coming from Jesus personally. We know He went into the desert to pray often but there does not seem to be much of what words He prayed.

I have often wondered about the prayers that Jesus was supposed to have said while in the Agony in the Garden. If the apostles were off and sleeping while Jesus prayed, who heard Him to be able to record His prayers? Did He tell the apostles later of what He prayed? Or is this possibly an addition by the gospel writer or maybe the translator? I don't really know because I am not much of a scholar. But I do believe that this is a pious add-on to show the humanity of Jesus.

As we know, all prayer is answered. Or so we have been told. But all prayer cannot be answered by God unless certain conditions are adhered to.

God's mercy and forgiveness are for all and will not be denied to anyone who has mercy and forgiveness for his fellow man. How can I receive God's forgiveness if my heart is not open to give it to others? Can I have God's ear as it were, if I do not have within me the capability of passing forgiveness on to other human beings? God cannot give to me what I cannot comprehend and give to others.

God is immutable, which means that He cannot change His attitude toward man because His Love is always there. Therefore, prayer cannot change God's mind. Prayer, then, changes man's attitude toward God. It is the intention or the motive of the one praying and his heart or internal disposition that allows us to gain entrance to the ear of God. Gaining the ear of God is not granted by social or repetitive prayers, or by any economic or religious attitudes beseeching God for something. We know that Jesus prayed often to the Father, but we do not know exactly how and what He prayed for. Whatever it was, at any particular time, had to be in keeping with His mission in the world.

That was to bring the knowledge of the Father to this world. It follows, in my mind then, that His prayers would be focused on what the Father wanted or willed Him to do, and that would be humanity as His primary concern. We know we are to pray in secret and not as the Pharisees did who concentrated more on themselves and not very much on others. It seems that we should pray more for our brothers in the world, that they will be able to receive God's Holy Spirit and His Love and, then, that same Spirit and Love will be given to us.

Prayer is of the soul and a personal matter between the individual soul and God the Father. It also seems that there is not much we can give God in prayer. The only thing that we can give God as humans is thanksgiving or gratitude. We have of ourselves nothing else to give. Thanksgiving will lead to true worship of the Father, which is the highest form of prayer. To pray out of a "want" will give us just what we are asking for – a "want". Pray out of abundance and we will receive abundance. This clears up in my mind what Jesus said, "To those that have, more will be given. Those that have not, it shall be taken away." This has always puzzled me because it seemed like a mean attitude on the part of the Lord. After thinking about it, I guess I was wrong again. Seems to be a habit with me.

The Veil of Words

Did you notice that words don't mean what they used to mean? I'm not really too sure if words have lost their meanings or if we, perhaps, don't trust them to mean what they were originally intended to mean. For example, after a commercial about a car there is a voice which sounds like a machine gun going full tilt which spews out words of a disclaimer about the car. It is complete gibberish and unintelligible and cannot be deciphered by the ear of the common person, or an alien for that matter. But I assume there must be a law behind it. Or perhaps, there may be a commercial about a certain drug, any drug for that matter, which primarily touts its effectiveness for the cure in question, but nonchalantly glosses over the serious side effects that may go along with it, side effects that may include death or disease more serious than the drug in question is supposed to cure. Just think about it.

Do we just suppose that we won't have an erection that lasts for four hours, because it isn't common? To what end (no pun intended)? A drug may cause blindness or blurred vision but what the heck, drugs are really safe. Ask the pharmaceutical company that sells it. Or better yet, ask your doctor. After all, the pharmaceutical company trained him. I ask: Is this about the meaning of words or words having no meaning, or is it about our naïve attitude toward those people who are ostensibly supposed to be helping us and protecting us?

Maybe the question should be asked: Is there a VEIL between THEM and US? A veil that allows THEM to say what they want whether it is truthful or not? A veil that developed because we want to trust THEM so much that we do not look deeper into what they are trying to sell US at any cost (and it is usually at our expense). Do we really look at what is being said and by whom and for what reason, or do we casually assume that they are telling the truth and we are too lazy to care whether or not it is true?

Have we become so immune to political babble that it is easier to listen and not care than to exercise our right to the truth? Have we given up the God-given right to question and care enough to speak out? Do we care whether the THEY are lying to the US? Maybe it is time to doubt and question those once-sacred corners of our society and culture.

Those four corners of our culture are: the media – science – educational system – and the drug companies. I have left out our Government on purpose. Most of US expect THEM to not tell the truth unless it is expedient for them. If this sounds cynical it probably is, but perhaps it is time to set aside our laziness, video games, and desires for all the material pleasures of life and look for TRUTH. THERE IS ONLY ONE PRINCIPLE – ONE POWER – ONE TRUTH – ONE GOD.

The Journey of a Renegade

Priest to God

"WE ARE MADE IN THE IMAGE AND LIKENESS OF GOD…TO KNOW HIM, TO LOVE HIM, AND TO SERVE HIM."
Baltimore Catechism.

I have recently read somewhere that when we were in eternity with God, before He created us and we came into this world, He asked us to do something in this world for Him. He asked us to be His hands and to reveal to others what He was…or at least do something on His behalf. Of course, we agreed to do it. I believe that I agreed also. The next thing that happened after agreeing to this was that I found myself in my mother's womb and began sliding down her birth canal! As is natural with all births that are normal, I came into this world crying. All babies cry upon birth. Why? Perhaps we forgot what we promised God that we would do for Him. What a bummer!

He did agree on His part to help us remember but we forgot that part too! Now the learning or re-learning process begins. From early on it seems to be a struggle to fulfill what it was that we were meant to do in this world. This is the beginning of the JOURNEY TO THE SOUL'S MAJESTY, the splendor of God's reflection in this world.

In Gregg Braden's series, "LEARNING THE LOST LANGUAGE OF GOD", he talks of the Dead Sea scrolls and mentions a scroll that was not found with the other scrolls, but found in the same area as the others. This scroll is six feet long and contains a thousand words, and is believed by some to have been written by Jesus, Himself. The first words of this scroll relate that when a man and woman conceive a child, that child from the first instant of its conception, has knowledge and wisdom of eternity. (Quite a difference from the Thomistic view of the early Christian philosophy.)

No matter what, it does seem that whether you believe in evolution or not, we as humans who have a consciousness that animals do not have, progress (sometimes with great difficulty) to a higher order or level of awareness. Since our prehistoric or caveman days we have become aware of a spirit or soul within us, a reflective consciousness as it were, of who we are and what we are to do, or at least, what we are to try to do. It is an awareness of the soul. It seems to be the natural order of mankind to become more conscious of himself through his cultural surroundings, education, and traditions handed down from generation to generation. It is not necessarily a miraculous progression of awareness, but one which seems to be a natural biological and psychological process. It is not necessarily linear, but sporadic in its growth, and in this present day seems to be accelerating more than ever at a pace that sometimes seems mind-boggling. I believe that this process of awareness is present in all of us if we give it our attention, which most of the time we do not.

We have become too busy with the material things of the world and have forgotten, a great deal of the time, that we are spirits having a human experience. Our journey, then, is to discover the magnificence for which we were created. I also believe that Jesus, being a true and full human being, underwent this same process. This is not to deny His Divinity any more than it is to deny that we possess a part of that same Divinity. After all, did we not all come from the substance of the Supreme Creator? Have we not come from the Mind of God? Perhaps, not in the same way that Jesus did, but do we not all have missions and reasons for our existence?

There is very little known about the early years of Jesus. After He was born He seems to have dropped out of the picture according to the Bible. We first become aware of Him in the Bible teaching the elders in the temple when He was twelve years old. His earthly mother and father had to be upset because they didn't know where he was. Didn't He tell them He was God and that they shouldn't worry about Him? That was a pretty big secret to keep from His family.

Again, from this time on in the biblical accounts we have, nothing is known about Jesus until around His thirtieth year. What was going on? Nobody seems to know and yet, at around thirty years old, here comes this person who is well versed in the cultural attitudes and religious attitudes of His day, and takes issue with them. How and where did He get His knowledge and awareness? Why did He say at twelve years old, that He had to be about His Father's business? Question...is this also a non-factual event to prove His Divinity by the gospel writer? HMMM. The question remains – would it have been more fully human for Jesus to become aware and conscious of His Divinity, not by direct angelic process, but by the process of introspection of self?

Richard A. Money

Yet, it can be argued that since angels are the messengers of God they brought the awareness to Jesus. Miraculously? Maybe. It is written in the gospels that Jesus often went into the desert to pray and to get in touch with His Father. Did the Father speak to Him in a booming voice, that since no one else was around He could not be heard, and only Jesus could hear Him? Think about it.

How did He get in touch with His Father (the word in Hebrew means Source)? Could it not mean that Jesus was discovering who and what He was and what He was to do by going within Himself? Would it not be more in keeping with the way the Supreme Creator works for Jesus, born a man to a man and woman, to become aware of what God's mission was for Him, and to remember that He was to reveal Himself as God Incarnate to all men?

As Jesus became more aware and conscious of His mission, He made choices that would reveal that mission to all in His day, and for all days to come in this world. His preaching would become the revelation of the Father to all men, which would make all men sons of that same Father, and brothers to each other, and also brothers to Jesus. Likewise, the manner of His death would be His decision to ensure that His message would be received and that His Resurrection would be a lasting event. His message was Eternal Life with God the Father.

The manner in which He died was not unique for His day, but it was the worst possible for the times. Would not His resurrection have an even greater impact?

What I feel we have forgotten is the fact that Jesus is a spirit and that we are all spirits, each of us having our own mission. Jesus was to reveal that He is the Christ. Ours? (Yet to be determined until passage back to eternity with the Father and Jesus.) Awareness and conscious awareness are spiritual qualities that we are all capable of putting into effect. To know what and who we are may take a lifetime, and usually does. It is an act of remembering, and as we remember, so does the world around us remember. It is an individual act and a very personal one. It is also both individual and collective. The self-consciousness, and self-awareness's of my life may not seem to be miraculous, but to me they are definitely the work of God. How He did it I will only know when I get back Home. As events and occasions have unfolded in my life, they may not mean much to the reader. But even though at the time I was not aware of their importance, as I recount them to myself in the present, their importance seems to emerge.

My Soul's Journey to the

Bridge

To be a bridge between Man and God has always been my deepest desire. There have been many detours along the way, but the game is not over. A detour is only a delayed outcome. Some things may come to pass, possibly in the near future, and some may not. Nevertheless, I know that what I am doing is what He wants me to do. It is up to Him. If the gift of physical healing takes place through me it will be the final step on the bridge of my life and my walk with the Lord. In all probability, it may be the culmination of my journey to my soul's majesty.